Praise for
Running on Full

"Real. Authentic. Raw. Mitch Harrison first reveals his own personal journey in and through burnout. From there, he shares the 'secret sauce' of the fight back to health and how YOU as a leader can intervene now to prevent burnout for yourself and those you lead. Whether you lead at home, in a huge business, or in a nonprofit, *Running on Full* is a must-read for anyone working to make an impact in the world."

—**Doug Parks,** Founder and CEO, Intentional Churches

"Mitch Harrison's *Running on Full* offers a vital blueprint for leaders to combat and prevent burnout. He provides practical strategies to help leaders show up at their best in every aspect of life. This book is essential for anyone committed to achieving peak performance and fostering a thriving workplace."

—**Sam Reese,** CEO, Vistage Worldwide

"*Running on Full* offers a refreshingly practical roadmap for avoiding burnout and maintaining energy for what matters most. Through his own compelling burnout story and recovery, Mitch Harrison provides a clear, actionable framework that helps readers identify their early warning signs and build personalized replenishment practices. This is essential reading for anyone who wants to stop merely surviving and start thriving."

—**Kyle Idleman,** Senior Pastor of Southeast Christian Church, author of *Not a Fan*

"The book you are holding lays out a roadmap toward life in all its abundance—should you choose to accept the challenge and pay attention to the wise steps offered by Mitch Harrison. With vulnerability as he describes his own journey, Mitch offers practical guidelines that can lead us to greater joy, less stress, and maximum peace. It's up to the reader to move from casual reading of good ideas to actual application that promises to make a difference. I urge you to dive in!"

—**Nancy Beach,** Leadership Coach, author of *Next Sunday*

"As I was reading *Running on Full*, I realized we don't pay enough attention to how we're living. We let ourselves 'drift' into a life that isn't good for us nor for the other people in our lives. Then, we feel guilty when we try fixing things that we can't even identify. Mitch's process and tools help us identify the warning signs that can keep us from 'running on full.' It's a terrific guide to help us avoid the consequences of a life out of control."
—**Stan Endicott,** Cofounder of Slingshot Group and The Grand Plan,
creative maverick, and mentor

"Few have given the amount of deep thought and practical tools for thriving and sustainability as Mitch Harrison. Born in real-life practice, he guides us from doable daily rhythms to deep-dives into the heart of us. This book gives us what we need to partner with the Spirit and live out our calling with full hearts and tanks!"
—**Drew Moore,** Lead Pastor, Canyon Ridge Christian Church

"Regardless of our roles, how do we get the most out of life and not lose our lives simultaneously? *Running on Full* takes a new approach to this old idea. Mitch's insights, recommendations, and life experience provide real-world solutions to real-world challenges."
—**Bob Day,** Chief of Police, Portland Police Bureau, Portland, Oregon

A PLAN TO BEAT BURNOUT AND
REPLENISH YOUR INNER TANK

RUNNING ON FULL

MITCH HARRISON

LEAFWOOD
PUBLISHERS

an imprint of Abilene Christian University Press

RUNNING ON FULL

A Plan to Beat Burnout and Replenish Your Inner Tank

Copyright © 2025 by Mitch Harrison

ISBN 978-1-68426-283-0 | LCCN 2025003763

Printed in the United States of America

Published in association with The Gates Group, 1403 Walnut Lane, Louisville, KY 40223.

LIBRARY OF CONGRESS CATALOGING-IN-PUBLICATION DATA
Names: Harrison, Mitch author
Title: Running on full : a plan to beat burnout and replenish your inner tank / Mitch Harrison.
Description: Abilene, Texas : Leafwood Publishers, [2025] | Includes bibliographical references.
Identifiers: LCCN 2025003763 (print) | LCCN 2025003764 (ebook) | ISBN 9781684262830 paperback | ISBN 9781684268177 ebook
Subjects: LCSH: Burn out (Psychology) | Burn out (Psychology)—Prevention
Classification: LCC BF481 .H373 2025 (print) | LCC BF481 (ebook) | DDC 158.7—dc23/eng/20250527
LC record available at https://lccn.loc.gov/2025003763
LC ebook record available at https://lccn.loc.gov/2025003764

Cover design by Outerwear
Interior text design by Sandy Armstrong, Strong Design

Leafwood Publishers is an imprint of Abilene Christian University Press
ACU Box 29138
Abilene, Texas 79699

1-877-816-4455
www.leafwoodpublishers.com

25 26 27 28 29 30 31 // 7 6 5 4 3 2 1

Contents

Introduction 7

1 How Are You Doing, Really? 19

2 The Balancing Act 33

3 The Unhappy Accident 45

4 The Real Problem 59

5 The Plan—Begin with Rest 77

6 Release 93

7 Receive 111

8 Recreate 127

9 Relate 141

10 Accidental Genius 153

11 Awareness Is Almost Everything 165

12 Good Living, Great Life 185

Introduction

Crash

I found myself staggering down the middle of the Las Vegas Strip one night. Head spinning. Struggling to stay on my feet. Pretty sure I was going to pass out.

No, it wasn't for the usual reasons people find themselves stumbling down the Strip.

I was running the Rock 'n' Roll half-marathon, and somewhere between miles eleven and twelve, the wheels came off. I went from feeling as good as I ever felt running a half-marathon to feeling as bad as I ever felt in my life. I thought, *If I keep going, I am going to pass out and end up in a medical tent.*

I couldn't figure out what had gone wrong. I had done all the recommended training. I had dropped weight before the race so I'd be lean and mean for the big day. And this wasn't my first half-marathon—it was my eighth. I knew how to do this. Surely I hadn't fallen victim to the rookie experience of hitting the wall. That's what happens to people who don't know what they're doing.

The worst part: I could see the finish line from where I was standing. It was taunting me, but I couldn't move. I stood by the side of the road leaning on a guardrail for a while—like *twenty minutes* a while. I stood there watching people I had worked hard to pass go by me like I was standing still—because I *was* standing still. Visions of putting up my personal best time vanished.

Finally, I remembered that my wife and three teenage boys were standing halfway between where I crashed and the finish. I had asked them to be there to cheer me on for the home stretch. Since my ego wouldn't let me walk past my boys—and I knew I'd never hear the end of it from them if I did—I hobbled my way into a jog and dragged myself the last mile and a half of the race.

Over the next days, I asked some runner friends what they thought had happened to me. After hitting me with some probing questions about my training plan, they finally settled on the simplest explanation. I didn't eat enough. In the week before and day of the race, I hadn't taken in enough calories to sustain me for the level of exertion that running 13.1 miles brings.

I simply ran out of fuel.

Not What, But How

The second time I found myself hitting the wall was in a hallway at work, between the human resources director's office and mine.

I crashed—metaphorically and almost literally. This time, it didn't threaten to take me out of a race; it took me out of work and much of life for six distressing months.

The ironic thing is that it never should have happened to me. That's what I thought, anyway.

I believed I was the least likely person to burn out. I had played high school and college football. I wasn't the biggest or strongest player, but I worked hard. If you needed intensity and determination, someone to keep going when it was easy to quit, I was your guy. I knew how to push myself and not give up. Turns out, those noble qualities of perseverance and tenacity have a shadow side that won't do you any favors when what you really need to do is rest.

Not only did I value resilience; I worked at a job that promoted personal replenishment and health. I was the executive pastor at a large house of worship in Las Vegas. Our church placed a strong emphasis on the well-being of everyone on our team. We encouraged our staff to take a weekly Sabbath—to set aside twenty-four hours to rest and intentionally not be productive. We also offered a paid monthly day away from the office for personal reflection, spiritual connection, and again, rest. Vacations were inviolable. When you were off, there was no requirement to check emails or stay connected to work. We also provided sabbaticals for our staff to step aside from work to recalibrate, recover, and yes, rest. Before I burned out, I had been in the organization long enough to have taken two sabbaticals.

I'll add what should be obvious: I worked for a church. I had a long-standing and well-developed (or so I thought) faith. I had the encouragement of my peers, my boss, and my friends in the congregation to live a life of joy and peace. If there was ever an environment that was conducive to not burning out, it was this one.

Perhaps that encourages you in some almost morbid way. You may be thinking, *If you had all that going for you but you burned out, no wonder I'm struggling! Because I certainly don't have that kind of supportive workplace.*

Yeah, I know.

You may be wondering, *If you had all that going for you, why did you burn out?*

As my son would say, "That is a fantastic question."

Looking back, I can see what was happening to me, and I can also see that my burnout was not about what was happening to me.

I left the human resources director's office, where we had just finished meeting about a formal complaint one employee had filed against another. I'll spare you the details, but it was a difficult and complex problem. Unfortunately, it wasn't close to the worst work-related problem I was facing.

An executive pastor in a large house of worship functions like a chief operating officer at a company. I oversaw a team of direct reports who oversaw every aspect of the organization. I thought of my job as keeping an eye on everything to make sure everyone was heading in the right direction.

One of my primary roles was to function as a sort of chief of staff, overseeing human resources functions, policies, and processes, and so there were always problems to handle and issues to untangle.

Looking back, it had been five straight years of challenge upon challenge, including employee conflicts, necessary terminations, and navigating a succession plan for the longtime iconic senior leader of the church. But the issues weren't just at the office.

During that same period, my wife discovered a lump that turned out to be fast-growing breast cancer. For an entire year, she was in treatment, which included chemotherapy, surgery, and radiation. That brought an emotional weight I had never experienced.

It wasn't any one of those issues by themselves that caused my burnout. Each of them, on their own, would have been heavy but manageable. Together, they were a lot.

But even all of them together wasn't the cause.

It wasn't what I was carrying that got me. It was how I was carrying it that ultimately did me in.

It wasn't what happened to me, but it was what was happening inside me, or more accurately, what wasn't happening in me, that took me down.

A Burnout Epidemic

You've probably faced difficulties that make my story sound painless by comparison. You may be in the middle of a season of struggle right now. Or it might not be any specific problem; it may just be your life that has you feeling overwhelmed and stuck.

Chances are that you've burned out, are in burnout, or are headed for burnout.

The numbers are numbing:

- In 2023, 43 percent of people from over one hundred countries complained of suffering workplace burnout.
- The American Psychological Association found, in a 2021 survey, that 79 percent of employees were experiencing work-related stress.
- Eighty-three percent of employees notice burnout negatively impacting their personal relationships.
- It may not just be job-related. While burnout is generally associated with work, many contend that it can also result from non-workplace stress.
- In fact, "55 percent of stay-at-home moms admit they 'always' or 'frequently' feel burnt out."
- In college students, the rate of moderate to severe depression rose from 23.2 percent in 2007 to 41.1 percent in 2018, while rates of moderate to severe anxiety rose from 17.9 percent in 2013 to 34.4 percent in 2018.
- Up to 60 percent of doctor visits today are due to stress-related issues.

Those statistics are sobering. I wonder if you find yourself in them? Are you on a collision course with burnout? Do any of these statements describe you?

- ► You don't really know how to rest.
- ► You enjoy feeling successful but feel like it means you can never stop working, and you hate what it's doing to you.
- ► You can't seem to turn off the neon light mental to-do list flashing in your head all the time.
- ► You stare at the ceiling—a lot—because you can't sleep.
- ► You've found yourself sitting in your car in your work parking lot because you don't want to face what awaits you inside.
- ► You've watched issues become endless and people become problems.
- ► You've gone to bed, and woken up, with a phantom anxiety that you can neither identify nor escape.
- ► You've felt the burden of having to produce more results and achieve more success while realizing that the expectations will never stop.
- ► You feel responsible for everything and enjoy nothing.
- ► You feel drained, trapped, empty, alone.
- ► You've become close companions with fatigue, distraction, impatience, and anxiety.
- ► You wonder if it will ever change, and if so, how.
- ► You can't see a future that doesn't include more of the same.

Whether you are a CEO or a stay-at-home parent, you are facing a lot every single day.

But perhaps the real issue is not what is happening to you. It's not what you're carrying, but it's how you're carrying it. The way you carry your burdens will be the difference between you thriving through difficulties or going down in flames.

If you don't do something soon, you could end up like I did in the hallway outside my office. And that is definitely not a place you want to be.

Disappear into a Fog

As I made my way back to my office, it hit me that I had felt this way once before—in the middle of the Strip just past mile eleven of the race.

I felt so empty I couldn't keep going.

It was like something inside of me had broken.

I had been tired and worn down before, but this wasn't an "If I just get some time away, I'll be fine" or "I don't know if I want to stay in this job" kind of moment.

It was like I was watching the road of my life evaporate into a fog in front of me. I thought, *This is how people feel when they do desperate things.*

The memories of how I felt that night at the half-marathon came flooding back. I was struggling to move forward. My head was spinning. I knew I couldn't keep going. I slumped into my chair and spent the next hour trying to figure out what was happening to me. But I couldn't put things into perspective, couldn't get it together, couldn't find the energy to rally one more time.

As I thought about where I was in life, I realized . . .

I was tired. Beyond tired.

I felt disoriented, like even familiar things were unfamiliar.

I had no joy in my life, just responsibility.

I was afraid of what might land on my desk next. I had lost perspective. Everything seemed bigger than it was. Even things that weren't problems looked like problems.

I felt trapped. I couldn't see a future that didn't include unbearable stress, but I didn't feel the freedom to walk away.

I was grieving. I felt a dark sadness that kept showing up as anger. I was deeply disappointed in people who had made choices that dumped draining responsibility on me. I hated that the organization I led and had always loved had become such a source of pain.

Fortunately, over the next days, I had people around me, including my new boss (remember the succession plan?), who noticed something wasn't right and gave me the freedom to figure out what it was, eventually including five weeks away from work.

It wasn't easy. I talked to friends and read books that all suggested going to a professional ("Go talk to a counselor") or a place ("Go on vacation to Hawaii"). At best, those would be short-term fixes. I needed a long-term solution. I had to develop a plan for a new way of doing life.

I signed up for a weeklong intensive process with a therapist who had been helpful to me in the past. Through the all-day sessions, he helped me understand and untangle what had happened to me. He got me thinking about a proactive life built on refilling rhythms instead of a reactive life where I was always responding to my circumstances in the same old way. He told me I needed a plan that matched the level and type of stress I was experiencing. That was revolutionary to me.

I also connected with mentors, friends, and family who let me talk as long as I needed.

I got away.

I spent time with my wife and kids.

I had encounters with God.

I rested. Really rested. Altogether, it took six months before I felt like a normal human being again.

A Blueprint

Finally, I returned, committed to living by new principles.

Those principles saved me. They provided me a blueprint to live by that kept me healthy and allowed me to be my best for my job and for the people who matter most. They have put me in a completely different place when it comes to handling stresses and warding off the early warning signs of burnout. Today, I'm living a different kind of life.

The principles have become so invaluable to me that it's hard not to talk about them. One day, I did exactly that in a group I attend of high-level business leaders who meet for peer-to-peer coaching and executive development.

They asked about my time off. They were fascinated with what having that much time off felt like and what it had done for me. They wondered what I learned. I shared the new rhythms I had built into my life to prevent burnout and explained I was putting the principles I learned into a workshop I might one day offer to overwhelmed church pastors. When the group asked me to do the workshop for them, I laughed. It wasn't ready, and besides, they were business leaders, not pastors. They insisted I get it ready and that they needed it as much as any of my church friends.

Two months later, I nervously presented my workshop to the group. When I was done, one of them said, "Mitch, everyone needs to hear this." The leader of our group said, "I'm going to start calling other groups to let them know this is available."

Since then, I've crisscrossed the United States teaching this blueprint that I call the "Refill Plan" to over one hundred groups and well over a thousand people—in less than two years. It's mind-blowing to me. The people I've taught it to tell me it's life-changing, and every time I teach it, I get more requests to share it with others.

And now I get to share it with you.

One of the themes found throughout the Bible is God's ability to redeem the troubling, awful, unfortunate circumstances of life and to bring beauty out of even our darkest and most difficult experiences.

Although my experience with burnout was bad—so dark and confusing it stopped me in my tracks—I believe God is now allowing me to use it for good. Hopefully, for your good.

Reading this book might just change your life. Putting the principles into practice definitely will.

As we go on this journey together, you will learn how a growing self-awareness is indispensable in managing your well-being.

You will also learn that avoiding burnout and showing up at your best requires an intentional plan that includes five rhythms:

- ▶ Rest—taking periods of time when you stop working
- ▶ Release—setting down the emotional weight you're carrying
- ▶ Receive—finding inspiration and expression of your most meaningful contributions
- ▶ Recreate—developing rhythms of life-giving times of enjoyment and fun
- ▶ Relate—connecting deeply with the people who fill your soul

Without any one of these, you could be in danger of a crash. These rhythms might seem obvious, and if they are, isn't that all the more reason to prioritize them as part of your regular habits? They may seem simple, but you'll find that applying them will cause you to have to reflect deeply and make choices that could make all the difference in your personal well-being.

You are going to get a step-by-step plan, but you'll also discover what I did: that a plan is necessary but not enough. We also need to identify and attack the depleting mindsets—toxic responsibility, chronic improvement, compulsive achievement, and hyper-urgency—that keep us from prioritizing our personal well-being. I'll show you how to do that.

As you learn how to overcome these depleting mindsets, you will become empowered to give yourself permission to stop working to exhaustion and start living in the restorative rhythms you need.

Keeping your tank full doesn't have to be a mystery. It does require intention and awareness. It turns out getting real rest requires some work on the front side. But it's worth it in the end. If you're willing to do the work, you will find yourself with all the capacity you need, no matter what race you're running or challenge you're facing. You'll show up at your best in the most important places and with the most important people in your life.

1

How Are You Doing, Really?

I might be superhuman.

No, really. Why, you ask?

I've been driving for over forty years and have never run out of gas.

If you haven't either, you are eligible to join me in the elite club of gas-tank ninjas.

I'm kidding, but it's true. I have never had the experience of ignoring the gas gauge to the point my car sputtered to a halt by the side of the road.

But I have been close.

Very close.

Years ago, I would play a game called "How orange is the light?" Have you played it? You play chicken with your low fuel light, letting it glow on your dashboard while you tell yourself, "It's not that orange."

Why would anyone play this game?

Because you don't want to stop and get fuel.

I've done it more times than I can count, but somehow, I've never run out of gas.

My wife and kids will get in the car, see the orange light, and ask, "Shouldn't you fuel up?"

I scoff at their ignorance.

I offer reassuring words like "I'm watching it" (even though I'm not), "I know how far I can go after the warning light comes on" (I don't), or "It'll be fine" (I've never known that for sure).

It becomes a matter of pride, like I can prove my manliness by seeing how long I can go before I stop.

The thing I've noticed is those rides are never fun. Turns out, playing Russian roulette with your fuel tank produces a fair amount of anxiety.

Yet I just keep pushing the limit, waiting as long as I can to do what I know I need to do to refill the fuel tank on my car. I realize one day this will catch up with me, but every time I coast into a gas station on fumes without completely running out of gas, my sick behavior is reinforced.

One of these days, I'm going to misjudge how much fuel I have left in the tank and run out before I can refill.

It has not happened yet in my car, but it's exactly what happened in my life.

Really?

"Fine." "I'm good. "Can't complain."

These are typical go-to answers we give to the deeply important question, "How are you doing?" The problem when we give these answers is that we don't really mean it.

I will stop short of saying we're lying. We just don't think much about the question before we answer. It feels like more of a greeting than an invitation to honesty.

I get it.

I ask people how they're doing all the time, and I don't usually mean, "Dig deep and reveal to me what's going on in the private recesses of your soul."

I mean, "Hi."

Why bring this up?

Because the answer to the *How are you doing?* question is deeply significant. Somewhere along the way, we should answer it truthfully. We need to pause and take a longer look at how we're actually doing—where we're struggling, what stresses we're experiencing, and what pain we're feeling. We should slow down enough to honestly assess how energized or depleted we feel. We need to answer the question truthfully.

How are you really doing?

Aware Enough to Assess

Here's a weird thought: Are you even able to give an honest answer to the *how ya doing* question?

I'm not suggesting you would lie. I'm asking if you'd even know.

If you said you were doing well, what is well?

And how would you know if you weren't doing well?

Your car comes equipped with an array of dashboard warning lights to inform you of what's going on under the hood. In your life, what indicators let you know you have all the fuel you need in the tank for all the responsibilities you are facing? Or if your tank is running low enough to warrant concern, if you're at a place where the next crisis could leave you empty, how would you know that?

It's not easy to measure our own personal well-being, but what's at stake—our mental health, the quality of our work and decision-making, the way we show up in our most important relationships—is way too important to not know.

After my season of burnout, I realized I would need to ask different questions and use different tools to get an accurate picture of how I was doing and avoid the same cycle of stress and collapse.

Instead of ignoring my inner world or flippantly responding to the "How are you?" question, I started asking, "How full is my tank?"

I'd ask myself: *On a scale of one to ten, with one being completely depleted and ten being completely replenished, how much capacity do I have to show up at my best in every place my best is needed?*

That is a good question. It's a good question in the same way these are good questions:

- ▸ What's the worst that could happen?
- ▸ How bad can it be?
- ▸ Can you hold it until we get to the rest stop?

These are questions that require a clear answer.

The problem I quickly ran into as I tried to accurately assess my number was that my optimism and determination clouded my perspective. I wanted to believe my tank was fuller than it was in reality. I was committed to acting like it was full no matter how I was feeling. Neither was helpful in getting to an honest assessment.

I also found I had a herculean ability to ignore or explain away moments when my true negative numbers broke through the always competent and always polished projection I showed the world.

When I was on the downward slide toward burnout, I didn't want to admit where I was headed. Truthfully, I knew I wasn't at my best, but where I was headed never crossed my mind. I'd always bounced back and recovered before. I had no reason to believe I wouldn't rebound again. I was blindly heading in the direction of a crash without any compass or guidepost to tell me differently.

I had developed a habit of denying my true condition. That habit was my Uber driver into burnout, and it was later my kryptonite when it came to assessing my status so I wouldn't burn out again.

When it comes to our personal replenishment, self-awareness is a big deal, perhaps the biggest deal. Your make-or-break skills are:

- ► Your ability to assess how you're doing with ruthless honesty
- ► Your awareness of what helps the most when you're feeling depleted

The issue is that most of us have little to no idea how we're doing or what can help, and ignorance is not and will not produce bliss. We assume we'll just drift toward feeling better, but the odds are better that we'll drift out to sea, at best feeling unmoored, and at worst having our personal Titanic-meets-iceberg moment.

Better Questions

In order to avoid burning out again, I had to ask better questions that would help me assess my true condition—questions like:

- ► What if my tank was full to at least an eight on a scale of one to ten?
- ► If my tank was that full, how would I know?
- ► What qualities would show up in me if my tank was legitimately 80 percent full?
- ► What qualities would tell me my tank was depleted to, say, three out of ten?

Why did I pick eight and three? Honestly, being at ten felt a little daunting. Even the gas tank on my car isn't completely full often or for very long. Just like the typical driving I do in my car drains the tank a little with every trip, the daily tasks and challenges I face also drain me a little.

I feared claiming that I was at ten might be the result of an ongoing lack of self-awareness or even self-deception. Besides, it seemed like the people who told me they were at ten all the time just wanted to be at ten and hoped saying it might make it true. Their "My life couldn't be better!" talk seemed aspirational and often a bit annoying.

I needed to know how I was really doing.

So do you.

Faking it is dangerous when navigating your personal well-being. You need a clear-eyed look at your personal gauges.

A recent study shows the percentages of people in the work-place who are "always or often" exhausted, stressed, overwhelmed, lonely, or depressed. The study shows the differences between what corporate-suite executives and other employees experience when they show up for work. Among the most alarming findings is that the most "encouraging" figure indicates that 23 percent of employees always or often struggle with some form of depression.

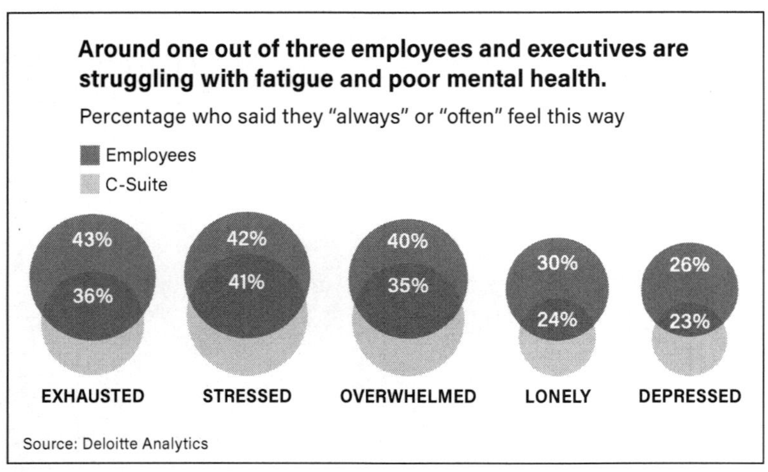

That's one in four. And that's the best finding; it just gets worse from there.

That's just how we are doing at work. We also need to accurately assess how we're doing at home. Unfortunately, this is another way in which we deceive ourselves. We somehow think we are two different people.

I've taught this material several hundred times to thousands of executives. They often tell me, "I'm an eight or nine at work, but I'm a three at home."

No, you're not.

Can you imagine a car saying, "I'm almost full in the city but close to empty on the highway." Sorry, car, but you are what you are, regardless of where you are.

The truth is, we take the same body with us everywhere we go. Underlying whatever face we put on at work, home, church, or with friends is the real level we're operating from in all those places. It may not feel that way, because the exhilaration of our work might seem to overshadow the demands of our home life (or vice versa). We can dress it up for a while or fake our way to the end of the day, but we take the same fuel tank with us everywhere we go.

Below you will find a simple tool to give you a more accurate picture of what you want to be all the time and help you assess how you're doing right now. Ask yourself:

What are the qualities that show up in me when my tank is full to about an eight?

________________________________   ________________________________

________________________________   ________________________________

________________________________   ________________________________

________________________________   ________________________________

What are the qualities that show up in me when I'm depleted to about a three?

_______________________________   _______________________________

_______________________________   _______________________________

_______________________________   _______________________________

_______________________________   _______________________________

After leading hundreds of marketplace executives, nonprofit leaders, and stay-at-home parents through this exercise, here are some of the most common responses:

E————How Full Is Your Tank?————F	
1———— **3**———————————— **8**———— **10**	
Irritated	Patient
Foggy	Creative
Anxious	Present
Apathetic	Flexible
Impatient	Joyful
Negative	Optimistic
Defensive	Resilient
Overwhelmed	Engaged
Sad	Calm
Agitated	Happy

Please pause here, and take another look at the lists.

Now, think again about the qualities that show up in you when your tank is full, to about an eight, or almost empty, to about a three.

Which of the qualities in the lists ring true for you?

What words on each of the lists resonate with your personality and experience?

Getting clear about your lists helps build an awareness of what you look like at your best and what you should watch for at your worst. This is the beginning of your ability to honestly and more accurately answer the question: "How am I doing, really?"

Three Critical Truths

Doing this exercise will reveal three critical insights you must know about yourself to beat burnout.

1. Less Means Less

Our inner fuel tank is not like the fuel tank of a car or the battery of a cell phone.

My car will function in exactly the same way regardless of whether the gas tank is just about full or almost empty. As long as it has any gas, it will not lose any of its capacity. If my gas gauge were broken, I would never be able to tell how much fuel I had based on the performance of the vehicle. That's why I can drive my car for a while and completely ignore the orange warning light that is screaming for my attention. As long as my car is working as it always has, why bother?

The same is true of a cell phone battery. When the battery level of your cell phone is at 10 percent, you don't lose the ability to use the Internet. Until it is completely empty, it will function in exactly the same way regardless of how much juice it has.

You are not like that.

The more drained you become, the more the negative "three" qualities start to show up. The less fuel you have, the less of those positive "eight" qualities you'll exhibit. You don't just run out of gas completely and then stop functioning.

Burnout creeps up on you. It doesn't hit all at once; it shows up a little at a time. And make no mistake, we're not the same at a five as we are at an eight. Simply put, we lose capacity and functionality the more depleted we become. If you're paying attention, you can see it coming.

2. Early Warning Signs

That points us to the second essential insight you need to beat burnout: your early warning signs. There are early warning signs that point to the possibility of a heart attack, pancreatic cancer, Alzheimer's disease, and even genital herpes (I don't want to know!). Similarly, we need to know the early warning signs of a depleting tank that leads to burnout.

Your early warning signs are the qualities that show up in you first when you start to get depleted. They are the initial indicators your tank may be running low. Think back to your "three" list—which of those qualities show up early to your "I'm going down the drain" party? What two or three characteristics do you notice first when fatigue sets in? Identifying these early warning signs allows you to detect your depletion early and begin to address it before bigger problems develop.

For me, it's irritation and anxiety. More specifically, it's easy irritation and phantom anxiety.

You may be familiar with the quick frustration and flash-paper anger that erupts when the simplest thing goes wrong. Yeah, that's me. When my tank is draining, if I drop my keys trying to unlock the car, if the Wi-Fi is slow, or if they get my order wrong at the drive through, then . . . "$%*#!"

And the anxiety? It's butterflies that show up in my stomach with suitcases and sleeping bags and hang around even though I have no idea why they're still there. I just know I'm worried about . . . something. I just can't seem to identify what that something is. I do know my pulse goes up, I get withdrawn, my normally helpful analytic skills go into overdrive, and I start to obsess.

How about you? What are your early warning signs? When you first start to feel fatigued, what are those ugly qualities that surprise you by peeking their heads out from behind the bushes? Don't know? An easy solution is to ask someone close to you—your spouse, kids, coworkers, close friends. Chances are, they've experienced your early warning signs in your tired and unguarded moments and see them earlier and more clearly than you do.

I cannot overstate the importance of identifying these early warning signs. If you do, you'll be able to detect and can address what's happening when you are still at a five or six. The truth is, it is way easier and takes way less time to recover from a five or six than from a two or three.

In this way, we are just like a cell phone battery—the more drained we are, the longer it takes to recharge. Too often, people keep going when they're down to a five, with the idea they'll grit their teeth and hang on until the vacation or long weekend coming in a few weeks. They assume they'll have sufficient time to recover then. It's only then that they find out how long it actually takes to recharge once they've hit a three. They manage to bounce back to maybe a five by the end of the vacation, and then they return to work with only a half-tank of fuel, only to stare at demands that require a full tank. Some find themselves on a perpetual rollercoaster ride, from a five to a three, then back up to a five, then down to a three again, then up to five, then . . .

Wouldn't it be better to see that our fuel is depleting when we hit five or six and then know how to recharge to eight or nine? You can live that life by knowing your early warning signs. They become your "low fuel" light so you can stop playing "It's not that orange" with your life.

3. True North

The third insight this exercise will reveal is your personal true north. Your true north qualities define who you want to be in the places and with the people who matter most. They describe you at your best.

To find your true north, look back at the words you thought described you at an eight. Which two or three qualities exemplify you at your best? Which ones are leading indicators, from which other good qualities seem to flow?

If someone told me, "When I'm present and optimistic, I'm more likely to also be creative, flexible, resilient, and engaged," I'd say, "Present and optimistic are your true north."

I will admit, these qualities can be more challenging to identify than our early warning signs. One method is to ask, "Which qualities are the opposite of my early warning signs?" Those might be your true north.

For example, I mentioned that my early warning signs are irritation and anxiety. My personal true north qualities are joyfulness and peacefulness—the opposite of my early warning signs. I've found that when I am characterized by joyfulness (the sense that what I'm experiencing is good and that more goodness is coming) and peace (an inner calming confidence that everything is going to be okay), then I am also able to be patient, engaged, flexible, and present.

Knowing our true north gives us the right target to aim at. Often our goal for a week is "just to get through it." We become so overwhelmed with pressure and stress that the best we can hope for is "just making it to vacation."

That's not the way we want to live our lives, and identifying our true north reminds us of who we really want to be. It points us in the direction of us at our best.

Take a look again at the list of common qualities of people at an eight. Those are the qualities you want in your employees, coworkers, and your kids' best friends. They define the people you hope will move in next door.

Frankly, those are the qualities your employees and coworkers, your next-door neighbors, your kids, and your spouse are hoping will show up in you when you walk in the door. But that will only happen when you are fully replenished. It took me a while, but I finally realized it was more than a little hypocritical of me to expect everyone else to show up like an eight when I wasn't showing up that way.

Knowing our true north qualities and early warning signs equips us with a framework to understand more deeply the answer to the simple question, "How are you doing?"

From that awareness, we will build a plan to help us be an eight more often than we're not.

How are you doing, really?

What's your real number?

I don't just mean today. You might feel great today. Then again, you are reading a book about burnout, so maybe not.

If you took an honest assessment of your life over the last three months, where would you land? How full is your tank? Is your little orange warning light on and getting brighter? Are people asking you when you're going to stop and refill your tank?

It does no good to try to make things sound better than they are, and there's no condemnation if things aren't as they should be.

It is what it is.

We are where we are.

But once we get clear about where that is, we can start moving to where we want to be. With a new plan, we can get on a new path and never again run out of gas.

2

The Balancing Act

Bad Guess

"Let's go on a road trip."

It sounded like such a good idea.

What I was thinking was, *Man, I'm really worn out from the pressures and responsibilities of work. You know what would be refreshing and helpful? Let's load our three young boys in the back of the minivan and head out for a* three-week *road trip to see the country. It'll be fun. It'll be refreshing. It will be full of idyllic moments at picturesque venues where we'll gather our family for a group hug as we stare off into the sunset.*

Good plan, right? We had a nice minivan that even had a DVD player in it. If the beauty of the open road ever got less than interesting for our angelic offspring, they could just pop in a movie to pass the time between our stops at the intellectually and emotionally engaging points of interest along the way. What could possibly go wrong?

You know what went wrong.

Three young and active boys cooped up in a minivan for long periods of time—movies or not—is a recipe for shenanigans and mischief.

One kid pokes his brother. Brother pokes him back. The first brother bumps the DVD player. It shuts off. "I was watching that!" A belching contest begins. Someone farts. Windows open. Everyone is yelling. Things are flying around the van. Things are flying out of the van. You know, a road trip.

Forty-five minutes into it, I was ready to kick everyone out of the van, walk away, and start a new life in an undisclosed location.

I was attempting to recover from the stress and exhaustion I had allowed to overtake me, so I took a wild guess at what might help. My best guess about what would help was woefully wrong. The time off added to my depletion rather than relieving it.

Ever done that?

You made plans for a much-needed vacation you counted on to refill the tank but only found yourself more tired when you returned. Then you found yourself saying what many of us say after an experience like that: "Now I need a vacation from my vacation."

Guessing is a bad plan when it comes to managing our physical, emotional, and spiritual reserves. We can't rely on guessing. We need to become experts at what refills our reserves.

The Critical Equation

It's no secret that if you want to be good at your job, good at a sport—good at anything—you'll have to give a fair amount of time and intention to developing the needed skills. Malcom Gladwell famously gave the ten-thousand-hour standard for becoming an expert at any task or discipline. Personal replenishment is no different.

Keeping your tank at an eight 80 percent of the time requires that we learn to do what many of us think we do naturally. We assume we know how to rest. We believe we're good at it. We're sure a couple of days off will equal all the recovery we need from a tough season. The truth is, we aren't born with an understanding of how to live a life of balance. There are skills we have to develop and competencies we have to master.

Specifically, when it comes to our personal replenishment, we need an equation to help us become masters at balancing. Just like running a half-marathon, to navigate the stress of work and life, we must carefully manage this equation if we are going to mitigate burnout and show up at our best.

Stress = Replenishment

Stress and replenishment must be equal.

When I think about my half-marathon experience, that just makes sense. I put myself through a huge amount of physical stress, and without enough replenishment, I experienced the full effect of what happens when the body runs out of gas. When I mismanaged the stress/replenishment balance that night at the race, I ended up standing by the side of road watching everyone else run the half-marathon I should have been running.

The same thing happened in my work; it just wasn't as obvious. Too much stress for too long, without the compensating amounts and types of replenishment, and I ended up sitting in my office contemplating the end of my job and maybe more. I felt trapped between the work I believed I had to do and the depletion that was telling me I couldn't keep doing it.

When the stress we're experiencing is greater than the replenishment we're receiving, it's only a matter of time before we run out of gas.

Stress/replenishment balance is a better equation to manage than trying to find the always sought-after but ever-elusive work/life balance. When people talk about work/life balance, most mean the right mix of time at work and time reserved to have a life they enjoy. That's typically measured in amounts of time. That's why many go looking for jobs with flexible schedules and adjustable hours of work so they have enough hours available for life. It seems these days that every poll of employees puts work/life balance at the top of the list of things employees are looking for in their jobs. Work-from-home policies are being written into most employee handbooks to address the demands of workers who want to spend one or more days a week working from home offices (or Starbucks, or the beach . . .). The trend that began as a necessity during the COVID-19 pandemic has become the norm in many industries in an attempt to help workers achieve this hard-to-define work/life balance.

It sounds like a good goal until you consider that life comes with a fair amount of work and stress we must account for as well. As it turns out, work that pays the bills isn't the only work we have to do, and the office isn't the only place that produces stresses that can deplete us.

Any parent of small children knows work doesn't automatically stop when you walk away from the office. Some of the most depleting work can happen the minute you walk in the door of your house to deal with "life"—in the form of toddlers, dishes, bills, and pets. Every stay-at-home parent knows work and stress don't require offices, cubicles, or warehouses. Also, as you get older, the responsibility of caring for aging parents, managing finances toward retirement, and dealing with your own health issues can also add to our load.

In one of my most challenging seasons of leadership, my wife and I took the trip of a lifetime to visit Israel. My parents had made it possible for the two of us and my brother and his wife to go with them and a group of friends from their church to visit the Holy Land. The timing felt great as the challenges of work mounted. It seemed like it would be just the break I needed from the pressures I had been experiencing. Because of my personal faith, I looked forward to this trip being a time of rest, renewal, and inspiration as I walked in the places Jesus walked. It was all of that. The time away from work was itself a great relief, and there were many deeply spiritual moments that touched me to my soul.

But one night, as we were preparing to get some sleep at a kibbutz by the Sea of Galilee, Nan told me she had found a lump in her breast. It had shown up suddenly and was growing almost daily. When she first noticed it, she didn't think much of it. But over time, it had grown to the point it was deeply concerning. That moment would send us into the thick of a battle with breast cancer (a battle she won, by the way!), which included chemo, surgery, and six weeks of daily radiation. That journey took exactly one year to the day from the time she told me about the lump by the Sea of Galilee until she finished her radiation treatment. She has been clear of cancer ever since.

The trip meant to check the "life" box also brought stresses we could have never imagined. Those new life stresses piled right on top of the work stresses that didn't go away just because I went on vacation for a couple of weeks. The thought of balancing work and life was not a helpful framework in accounting for the demands both work and life had made on me.

It Goes Both Ways

This equation works the other way too.

When we get too much replenishment and not enough of the right kind of stress, it can lead to burnout of a different kind.

Of course, some of you are asking, "Is there such a thing as too much replenishment?" Sounds like a fantasy, doesn't it? You might be thinking, *I'd like to try that on for a while!* But it is possible to over-replenish ourselves into a state of lethargy and languishing that is equally hard to recover from.

Think about it this way: Why do the parking lots at every gym in the country fill up in January? It's because we look in the mirror and realize we got way too much "replenishment" last year—or at least over the holidays—and it's starting to show. We notice we're not feeling as sharp and energetic as we've felt in the past.

What do we do? We head down to the gym looking for some stress! We sign up and pay money to have someone add some of the right kind of stress to our system. We get one of those stationary bikes with the monitor on it that connects us to other people who evidently didn't get enough stress last year either and to that guy with the microphone whose job (and apparent joy) it is to add all the stress we can endure.

With too much replenishment, we feel sluggishness set in to both our bodies and our brains, so we go looking for a challenge. We do this because we know—in some mysterious way—that adding some stress will help us find needed refreshment and reenergizing. We add stress to gain replenishment.

There are other versions of too much replenishment.

At the end of a long and exhausting week, have you ever determined the best remedy was to do nothing all weekend except binge-watch that Netflix series you've been wanting to catch up on while keeping your favorite pizza shop in business? Or maybe you've curled up with your laptop and phone to doomscroll the weekend away? We've even coined a term for this common behavior: bed-rotting. Somewhere in the course of a weekend like that, what started out as restful became anything but renewing. We got too much of a good thing.

An even more damaging version of this shows up when we add less than helpful types of replenishment to the mix, meaning alcohol or drugs. While there is nothing wrong with stopping by your favorite watering hole to have a drink with some friends after a long day of work or melting into the couch with a nice bowl of ice cream to unwind from the pressures of the day, doing that every day and in increasing amounts will eventually lead you away from the true replenishment you sought in the first place. Some have reached for artificial stimulants to help them feel more energetic and alert, only, over time, to experience the law of diminishing returns and to pay the price of feeling more depleted and empty than when they started.

Another kind of over-replenishment happens postretirement. A couple of years ago, I was speaking to a group of executives in the Midwest. As I made arrangements for the engagement with the leader of the group, he told me there was one person who would be attending the workshop he particularly hoped I could help. He described how one CEO in the group, who had spent many years building a fantastic business, had just sold the business to another firm as he headed into retirement. The new firm so respected this now-former CEO and the quality of his character they asked him to stay on for a while to help make the ownership transition smoother and to help the new firm retain the employees he had nurtured all those years. He agreed.

But now, he was lost. The group leader told me this former CEO would show up at the firm he used to own, chat for a while with his former employees, and find a couple of things to do here and there, but he was struggling and depleted. He had lost his sense of purpose. He hadn't found the next thing worth giving his time and energy to, and his energy had all but faded. He had made a lot of money when he sold the firm. He had plenty of free time on his hands. He had so many opportunities for replenishment that he was showing more and more symptoms of a unique type of burnout, the kind that comes from feeling that life has too little meaning. I realize that's not the way we typically think of burnout, but he was burned out on too much replenishment.

There's a narrative many from my generation grew up with about the plight of our dads who had spent their whole lives working: "When Dad retires, he better find something meaningful to do, or he'll be dead in five years." There is an alarming suicide rate among older men facing or living in retirement.[1] There is a unique kind of burnout that shows up when we lose our sense of purpose and meaningful contribution. This isn't just for retirees. Burnout from a lack of purpose can happen to any of us.

When we mismanage the balance between stress and replenishment in either direction, we're in danger of experiencing the exhausting effects of burnout.

How Much and What Kind?

Balancing stress and replenishment is the key to avoiding burnout and filling our tank so we can show up as the best version of ourselves. But to do that, you have to match the amount and type of stress and depletion you're experiencing with the amount and type of replenishment you're receiving. Both amount and type are critical to getting the balance right.

During my season of burnout, I went to see a fantastic counselor named John. I spent a week with him in his Florida office unraveling what had happened to me and working on a plan that would help me recover and never repeat the outcome. He told me I needed a plan of replenishment equal to the demands on me. He warned me it would probably cost me some money, some time, and some experimenting.

He explained how, in earlier years when he lived and worked in Colorado and his counseling practice began growing, the demands on his time, attention, and energy would leave him exhausted by the end of the week. Then a friend invited him and his wife to come to Florida for the weekend and use his boat as a getaway to refresh and recover. John took him up on it. They found it so refreshing and helpful that they eventually bought their own boat and moved their entire counseling operation to Florida. If he was going to be at his best for the kind of contribution he was to make in the world, finding the right kind of replenishment to meet the amount and types of stress he was facing was a top priority.

You may not be able to afford a boat or a relocation to Florida, but don't miss the seriousness and intentionality we must apply to recognize and address our need to match the amount and type of stress with the appropriate levels and types of replenishment.

It's difficult to put a tangible measurement on the amount or type of stress you're under or how much or in what way a particular responsibility, event, or action takes out of you. I wish I could give you a silver bullet secret that would pinpoint exactly what you need. There are stress assessments available for free on the Internet that can be helpful. But ultimately, the journey to clarity about what your specific replenishment needs are and matching them to your unique set of stresses and demands will take some experimenting, some self-awareness, and maybe even some money. But the more you practice, experiment, and notice, the better at it you'll become.

The first time I ran a half-marathon, I had no idea how long it would take to recover enough to run again with the same or greater strength. Endurance running at that distance has unique challenges only experienced in the running. People can tell you about their experience, but you won't know it for yourself and sense how your body and mind are affected until you lace up your shoes and get a few miles into the run.

I also noticed every race was different. Some courses were flat. Some went up and down hills. Some were mostly downhill.

Others, mostly up. Sometimes, the weather was calm, and other times, I would fight the wind all day. On top of that, I was different each time too. Other factors in my life would affect my energy, readiness, and mindset. All of this added to or subtracted from the energy it would take to complete the race. Each factor affected me differently than others. It took me running a few races and enduring many training runs to get a sense of how much recovery I needed and what type of recovery tools would help most.

For example, two days before a half-marathon I was to run at Disneyland, I got food poisoning and found my body evacuating itself of everything I had eaten in the past month, or so it seemed. I ended up dehydrated, undernourished, and exhausted from lack of sleep. I had to decide quickly if I was going to attempt the race. As soon as I felt able, I began rehydrating and eating as much as possible, knowing I wouldn't get all the normal prerace nutrition. I felt like I could run; I would just have to run differently. I set a different (slower) pace, and I walked through the hydration stations to take in more fluids during the race, something I had never done. I carried and consumed more gel packs for added nutrition. Most of all, I adjusted my expectations to keep myself from pushing harder than was wise. After the race, we were set to spend the day at Disneyland. Normally, even after a race like that, I could walk the park all day with no issues. On this day, I spent a lot of time finding benches and shady spots to rest. It was a different kind of stress that required a different kind of replenishment.

With running, there are principles and frameworks that are helpful guides. There is no shortage of people who are more than happy to offer their opinion, product, ritual, and routine to help you figure it out. But at the end of each race, I still had to figure out what worked for me.

To put together a good recovery plan for races, I had to learn to pay attention to how each race was affecting me.

Getting the stress/replenishment balance right is a lot like that. There are helpful principles and frameworks that can help guide us (this book will give you such a framework.) We can learn from others who are running this race with us, but striking the right balance requires a growing awareness of how stress affects us and what types of rituals and rhythms are the most effective in helping us recover. What is most effective for you is what is most effective for you. You may be wondering, *But are you going to help me figure out what is most effective for me?* Yes, we'll definitely get to that. And you can begin even now by starting to tune in to how different stresses affect you and what types of renewing habits help you recover.

What's the Big Deal?

We started this chapter saying we'd need skills and competencies to balance stress and replenishment so we could show up at our best. I often say in my workshops that we should become as competent and skilled at this as we are at our jobs.

I realize that might sound a little overstated. Of course, a guy like me who travels around speaking and coaching leaders and organizations on the importance and impact of replenishment plans would say something like that. But hear me out.

The best thing you could do for your business, church, or organization is to show up as an eight 80 percent of the time.

The best thing you could do for your family is to show up as an eight at least 80 percent of the time.

If you run a company, pastor a church, lead a nonprofit, or oversee a government agency, you know the best thing your employees or staff could do for your organization is to show up as an eight 80 percent of the time. You'd hope that was true, but in the Gallup "State of the Global Workplace: 2023 Report," it was found that in the United States and Canada, only 31 percent of workers said they were thriving at work. That's only three in ten! Over 50 percent of employees admitted they were "quiet quitting"—meaning they were doing just enough to not get fired. And 17 percent said they were "loud quitting" or were actively disengaged from their job. Almost seven in ten of all workers in the North American workforce were phoning it in, or worse.

The best thing any of us can do for the people around us in the places we go—whether it's at work, in our homes, in our churches, in our communities—is to show up at our very best most of the time.

EMPLOYEE ENGAGEMENT		
Based on the Gallup poll for 2023		
THRIVING AT WORK	QUIET QUITTING	LOUD QUITTING
% Engaged Regional	% Not engaged Regional	% Actively disengaged Regional
31%	52%	17%

If that's the best thing we can do, then guessing how to do it is a bad plan. I guessed a road trip would bring me replenishment. It didn't. You've also probably made guesses like that. Your personal replenishment and well-being are not things you can afford to get wrong.

Learning to master the balance of stresses that drain us and the replenishment that fills us could be among the most worthwhile skills you can acquire. This skill will show up in the form of a plan. That's where we're heading next.

NOTE

[1]Sharon Jayson, "Why Older Men Are Killing Themselves at Alarming Rates," AARP, November 28, 2023, https://www.aarp.org/health/healthy-living/info-2023/suicides-rising-among-older-men.html.

3

The Unhappy Accident

Sometimes, good things happen by accident. But not very often.

Sure, penicillin, Velcro, and the microwave oven were all stumbled upon, but most things we call an accident don't end up well.

Example: me learning how to ski.

I was about twenty-seven years old, and a group I was leading decided they wanted to go on a ski trip to Heavenly Valley, California. It would be a great group outing. We'd have time to bond, make some memories, and have fun.

Turns out, they were right—about the "making memories" part.

Did I mention I had never been skiing?

Of course, being twenty-seven has a way of talking you into things you'd do best to talk yourself out of. My thought process went something like, *Why wouldn't I be good at this? Just because I've never done it before doesn't mean I'll be bad at it. I mean, I'm an athlete . . . was an athlete. I'll just act like I know what I'm doing.*

How hard can this be? (Those are questions it's better to have an answer to in advance.)

Then I had the thought that would define the entire trip: *I'll just figure it out on the fly.*

Off we went. The first stop after we arrived at the mountain was the rental shop. I got fitted for the boots and skis, promptly went outside, and put them on. I slid my skis back and forth a few times to, you know, get the hang of skiing. It all seemed pretty easy. I was good to go.

My plan was to use the time between the rental place and the lift to sharpen what I was pretty confident was the right mix of natural coordination and athletic ability into the stuff of a decent enough skier. I made it to the lift line with no incident, and I even made what I thought was an amazingly graceful move onto the lift. I hopped right on there like I'd done it my whole life. *See? This is what I meant by figure it out on the fly.* So far, the plan was working great.

I had no idea where this lift was going, mind you. I knew nothing of different levels of ski runs or types of terrain. I was just enjoying the ride. Evidently, this ride was going to Canada. It was the longest, highest ski lift I had ever seen. In fairness, it was the only ski lift I had ever seen. But it was long. And did I mention high? I had no idea where we were going, but I was about to find out.

What I found out was that I had no business being on that lift.

When we got to Canada—it might not have been Canada— and it was time to exit the lift, I did not get off as gracefully as I got on.

I fell immediately.

Right in the path of all the other skiers trying to get off the lift. They had to stop the lift and wait for the new guy to figure out how to stand up in skis he had just put on for the first time at the rental place. They didn't go over "getting up in skis" at the rental place, perhaps because I was employing my "act like I know what I'm doing" tactic. For future reference, that's never a good plan.

When I finally managed to get up, I found myself heading down a steeper hill than I was prepared for—not that I was prepared for any hill—and I didn't know how to slow myself down, or stop for that matter. (Again, maybe they should have covered all of this at the rental place?)

I was suddenly moving faster than I had ever before without the aid of a motorized vehicle. My friends saw what was happening and started yelling "snowplow!" I took that to mean I was about to be run over by snow removal equipment. They meant for me to point the tips of my skis together in a V, like a snowplow, to slow myself down. Since I didn't know what they meant or how to do it, I figured out another way of slowing down—falling. I did that, which, by the way, hurt a bit more than falling down getting off the lift.

Somehow, I got back up, progressed forward, and realized I hadn't even yet made it to where the actual ski runs began. When I did, I discovered they were marked with symbols I remember looked like playing cards—except in the decks of cards I was familiar with, the diamonds were red, not black. And yes, I found out later that, in skiing, black diamond means, "You should not be here if you've never done this before." There's more than one way to find that out. I found out the hard way.

Let's just say I spent the next couple of hours experiencing the full effect of my "I'll figure it out on the fly" strategy. I learned a lot about the relationship between gravity and acceleration, as well as the meaning of the "coefficient of friction."

Life lesson? Figuring certain things out on the fly is a really, really bad plan. Trying to navigate a complex activity that can potentially lead to personal injury without the benefit of a thought-out plan can lead to painful outcomes.

But we do it all the time.

It's what led to my burnout.

Attempting to balance the complex relationship between the stress I experienced and the replenishment I needed without a plan is what led to my crash.

You may have experienced the same thing.

The Inconvenient Truth

Read this slowly: You rarely drift in a good direction.

One more time: You rarely drift in a good direction.

Ships don't drift into the harbor; they drift into rocks. Athletes don't drift into world-class shape; they drift out of it. Marriages don't drift toward intimacy and togetherness; they drift toward isolation and separation.

We don't drift toward replenishment. We drift toward depletion.

Being at an eight 80 percent of the time requires a plan. Ending up at a three most of the time happens by accident.

No one intends to end up depleted and drained. Zero people woke up this morning and said, "Today I'd like to make it my goal to be irritated, exhausted, unfocused, and apathetic! That will get me all the good I'm looking for! Yeah, let's try that!"

We don't plan to burn out—we drift into it.

Entropy is a thing.

Entropy is the thing that makes all energy run down toward decay. It takes what is orderly and organized and reduces it to chaos and disorganization—unless an intelligent force acts on it. That's how your teenager's room ended up looking the way it does. You made them clean it up. It was orderly and organized. But over time, it degenerated into disorganization and chaos because no intelligent force was acting on it (no offense to your very intelligent teenager).

We can all agree that the world is broken, at least in the sense that energy eventually runs down to decay. There is no such thing as perpetual motion, either in physics or in you. The drift is always in the direction of depletion. If we're going to regain that energy, we need a plan for recovery. It does not happen by accident in physics or in you.

If it seems like I'm hammering on this obvious point a little too long, it's only because we don't always act like it's obvious. We typically live like we can keep going indefinitely, or at least until the weekend. Then we'll just crank it back up, do it all over again, and assume all the energy we need will always be there. Why not? Youthful enthusiasm and resilience have always saved us before; why wouldn't they save us again? We didn't need a plan back then; why would we need one now? We've always been able to count on our wits, grit, and ability to rally to keep us moving. Our ability to recover always brought us back from whatever drained us.

When you've got all that going for you, who needs a plan for replenishment?

Turns out, we all do.

I've found that people who follow the teachings of Jesus, as I do, may be even more prone to this mistaken perspective. Why? Because we believe God will give us all the energy we need to do everything we have to do! Prioritize rest? Nah, God's got this!

Except . . .

Even Jesus rested.

It seems it was part of his plan. And why wouldn't it be? It was part of the grand plan of creation since the beginning. Six days to work. One day for complete rest.

If there was ever a person who had immediate and unlimited access to all the resources of heaven, I'd say it was Jesus. Yet even he took regular, intentional moments away from the demands of his work to rest, reset, and receive from his Father for the purpose of being ready for the work that lay ahead of him.

I find that so instructive for us.

Replenishment Requires a Plan

My bathroom sink has two drains in it. So does yours. It's built that way so it won't accidentally overflow. Someone planned for the possibility the drain in the bottom might get clogged or accidentally left closed while the water was left running. To keep the sink from spilling water all over the bathroom floor, there's another drain along the top edge of the sink to let the water escape even with the main drain closed. Because of that, it's very hard to overflow a bathroom sink. You would almost have to do it on purpose.

We have the opposite problem.

You have drains all over the place. Whether related to your work, home, kids, extended family, finances—there is no shortage of things that empty out your energy every day.

The difficulty we face isn't in finding ways to keep our abundant energy from overflowing; it's about trying to keep our "sink" from emptying out.

To keep your two-drain bathroom sink perpetually full or even overflowing, you would need a constant flow of water pouring into it. You'd have to figure out how to keep that water flowing in no matter what day, week, month, or year it was. You would need to make sure your water delivery system was working well and the bill was always paid. If you turned off the water, the sink would soon run dry. To keep it full, you'd have to do it on purpose. You'd need a plan.

Our personal replenishment works much the same way. In the last chapter, we said we need a constant flow of things that replenish us to match the amount and type of things that drain us.

That requires a system. Before my season of burnout, I always believed I could wing it, that I would just figure it out on the fly. Much like my experience with downhill skiing, it cost me a crash and a bunch of near misses to figure out that "on the fly" didn't cut it. I did just enough to keep a little in the tank, but when new drains were added or the existing drains got bigger, I had no margin to absorb it.

The issue with handling replenishment on the fly is that you can't predict the future. You have no idea what drains will show up. A plan for personal replenishment isn't about responding to whatever shows up; it's about preparing ahead of time to build margin for whatever comes your way. It's about building systems that fill your tank and provide an emotional, physical, mental, and spiritual buffer so you can absorb the drain without becoming completely depleted.

James Clear, the author of *Atomic Habits*, says, "We don't rise to the level of our goals. We sink to the level of our systems."[1]

Wanting to stay replenished and show up at our best is a good goal, but it isn't the one that saves us. In his book, Clear says goals almost don't matter. He notes that every NFL team has the goal of winning the Super Bowl. It's not the goal that differentiates the also-rans from the Super Bowl champs. It's the system.

The question is, do you have a good system? Have you been relying on a series of one-offs to try to maintain enough well-being to get by, or do you have a plan of regular habits and rituals that are delivering all the replenishment you need to stay ahead of the things that are draining you?

Do you have a good system?

For many, the answer is no.

For a long time, that was my answer.

I had served churches in leadership roles for years and had all the encouragement and resources necessary to put a plan together. I just never put it together. The church I was serving when I burned out had a very robust list of replenishment-oriented practices and a culture that encouraged team members to take care of themselves, and it held team members accountable for taking care of themselves. I remember telling prospective staff members they would be in more trouble for not taking vacation time than for taking too much time off. As I've mentioned, the church offered its full-time staff members sabbaticals—up to three months for every six full years of work completed. I took days off. I took vacations. I took the occasional "prayer and fasting" days offered for spiritual reflection and rest. I had been on two sabbaticals.

The problem was that even though I did some things that could have been helpful to me, they weren't part of a bigger plan that built toward recovery and health. They functioned as one-offs, never adding up to the kind of replenishment I actually needed for the long haul.

I knew I needed to do all these things; I just didn't fully understand what I needed from all these things.

Behind the Curtain

You might be wondering why I've spent so much time in this chapter making a case for building a replenishment system. Because after speaking to hundreds of CEOs, business leaders, corporate teams, church leaders, homemakers, and retired people, I've discovered that no one has a plan. Worse, many don't think they need one. In spite of their exhaustion, anxiety, and feelings of being overwhelmed, almost everyone is convinced that a couple of days off here and there and a vacation now and again will keep their tank full.

I thought this way too. And winging it worked, right up until it didn't.

Somewhere along the way, youthful enthusiasm, resilience, and energy gave way to reality. The drains were too many and too large for the minimal attention I was giving to my well-being. The people and responsibilities I wanted to give my best to were getting anything but the best of me. Finally, the crash of full-blown burnout told me I could no longer handle my stress in the same way I had before.

I've also discovered that many people don't have a plan because they don't know what the plan should include. Too many options and a sea of helpful hints became overwhelming. "Get some rest" doesn't cover it, and "take time for yourself" isn't specific enough.

You need an explicit plan that will guide you to what we all need but that can also be customized to support what you uniquely need.

The Birth of the Plan

In the process of recovering from my burnout, I stumbled on just such a plan.

I mentioned the church I worked for offered sabbaticals to its team members to get extended rest and recovery. One of my responsibilities at the church was to oversee personnel functions and policies, including those that facilitated sabbaticals. I began to meet with each person who went on sabbatical to make sure they had a good plan for how they would use their time. We'd talk for a while about their plans, and, inevitably, they would ask what I thought made a good sabbatical. Thinking back on my two sabbatical experiences, I found myself telling people the same five things:

1. **Get some rest.** "Rest is elusive and individual, so figure out what's restful to you, and get some of that."

2. **Unpack your emotional bags.** "I'm sure there's emotional baggage you've either brought with you or picked up along the way. Get with someone who can help you sort it out and appropriately unpack it."

3. **Reconnect with your calling and purpose.** "Search your soul, listen to God, reflect deeply. Do what's needed to rediscover what gives your life and work passion and meaning."

4. **Have some fun.** "Do things that make you laugh out loud and smile until your face hurts. You need joy, so find and do things you enjoy. Don't see this as an add-on. It's as important as all the others."

5. **Get with some people you dearly love.** "Find the people who refresh your soul, and spend some high-quality time with them."

I would end, "Do these things, and you'll have a great sabbatical," and then I would have them check their sabbatical plan to make sure it included all five elements.

One day, the lights came on.

These are the things we need all the time, not just once every six years on an extended leave from work.

When I was coaching our staff, the five elements I suggested were just a personal hunch. But the more research I read about the causes and cures of burnout, the more I discovered every piece of advice given and the conclusions of every study on the topic landed in one of these five categories:

1. **Rest:** Rest means finding time when you shut off your work and remove yourself from what drains you. It's exactly what we do when we sleep. Resting is all about shutting down the system for a while so you can recover and come back stronger. Aside from sleep, each person has their own unique way to feel rested.

2. **Release:** Emotional baggage creates emotional weight that takes energy to lug around. Some of that weight— like the weight of grief—you may carry for a lifetime. Some of it—like the sting of criticism—needs to be forgiven and left behind. Either way, you need practices that allow you to reflect on what emotional weight you're

carrying and find people with whom you can process these burdens and deal with them appropriately.

3. **Receive:** Living with purpose is fundamental to your well-being. You need purpose in life like you need air to breathe. People can do desperate things when their sense of purpose and meaningful contribution evaporates. While rest and release stop the drain of energy, receiving inspiration around your purpose adds fuel to the tank. Finding your white-hot "why" will keep energy continually flowing into you.

4. **Recreate:** You need to have fun. There's an old adage about what happens when you're "all work and no play." Recreation is about the things we do for the sake of enjoyment. When they get ignored, joy disappears. Too often, the more serious the responsibilities you add, the less recreation and fun you have.

5. **Relate:** Nothing can replace the goodness of deep friendship and relationships. We were made to connect with others—to know and be known. We're told in the Bible that "It is **not good** for the man to be **alone**" (Gen. 2:18—emphasis mine), and it's been confirmed in study after study. When you make time for people who know you, see you, empathize with you, and love you, you are restored and renewed on a soul level for which there is no substitute.

These are the building blocks of a replenishment plan that will help you avoid burnout and show up at your best. They are the keys to keeping your tank full.

But before you move too fast, these building blocks also need a context. Staying replenished is more than just knowing what we need; it's also about knowing how often we need it.

It's probably safe to say that all five of these have crossed your mind at one time or another as something you require to keep your tank full. None of them are mind-blowing. "Who knew I needed some rest? I'm shocked!" said no one ever.

It's the combination of finding the specific things we need from each category and the right frequency of doing them that makes this replenishment framework powerful.

For each of these five categories, you need to know what you should do and how often you should do it. What's the right frequency?

For each category, what are the right rhythms (daily, weekly, monthly, periodically [every three to four months]), or annually?

The kind of rest I require daily is different from the kind of rest I need monthly or annually. What I need from a day off is different than what I need from a vacation. Daily recreation—maybe walking the dog or riding your bike—isn't like a periodic, long weekend trip to the coast. Each meets different replenishment needs.

From the two perspectives of what you need and how often you need it, you craft a plan to meet your replenishment needs.

Don't Forget the Target

There's an old story told about a little boy who was given a bow and arrow for his birthday. He promptly went around to the back side of the barn where no one could see and began shooting arrows into the side of the barn. A while later, his dad went looking for him and found him still shooting arrows. Much to his dad's surprise, all of the arrows were stuck in the bullseyes of several targets the boy had painted on the barn. The dad was amazed at his son's accuracy. He asked, "Son, how did you get so good at shooting arrows in just a couple of hours?" The boy replied, "Well, first I shot the arrows, and then I painted the targets around them later."

Many people approach their replenishment the same way.

They take their best shot at it and call whatever they got a bullseye, thinking something like, *I guess that's as good as it's going to get.*

No. It isn't.

You can't forget the target when building a plan for your personal replenishment. How do you set the target? With the true north and early warning signs we talked about in Chapter One.

When I started using the five R's to build my plan, I knew I didn't want to ever burn out again, but there had to be more than just not burning out. I wanted to show up as my best self so those around me—whether they be family, coworkers, or even strangers—would experience the best of me, not the scant leftovers. I didn't want to just avoid "the bad"; I wanted to be "the good." Any plan worth building and doing must help me avoid my early warning signs and have more of my true north—less irritation and anxiety, more joy and peace. If the plan didn't accomplish that, it wasn't a good plan.

In short, the plan becomes an exercise in asking: What do I need, and how often do I need it, so I get more of my true north and less of my early warning signs?

A Tool

Below is a simple tool I developed to help us form and capture our plans. Putting the plan on paper is a critical step. Just like it's a bad idea to try to keep track of your checking account balance in your head, it's an equally bad idea to try to balance stress and replenishment without writing it down. This tool lets you see your true north and early warning signs so you can ask, "What do I need to get more of my true north and less of my early warnings?"

We will walk through the elements of this tool in the next chapters, and we will learn how to use it to put together the kind of plan that will serve you in balancing your stress and replenishment needs.

MY REFILL PLAN

REFILL COACHING

	REST	RELEASE	RECEIVE	RECREATE	RELATE
DAILY					
WEEKLY					
MONTHLY					
PERIODICALLY					
ANNUALLY					

EARLY WARNING | TRUE NORTH

REST
WHAT MAKES YOU FEEL RESTED? WHAT ARE THE PERIODS OF TIME YOU WILL NOT WORK?

RELEASE
WHEN WILL YOU REFLECT ON WHAT YOU ARE CARRYING? WHO WILL YOU UNPACK WITH?

RECEIVE
WHAT ADDS INSPIRATION, MEANING, AND PURPOSE TO YOUR CONTRIBUTIONS?

RECREATE
WHEN WILL YOU HAVE FUN, LAUGHTER, ENJOYMENT, ADVENTURE, EXERCISE?

RELATE
WITH WHOM WILL YOU FIND CONNECTION, EMPATHY, PERSPECTIVE, FRIENDSHIP?

It's simple, but I guarantee it's not easy. It will take some soul-searching, paying attention, and experimentation to determine the right things in the right rhythms that will help you live at an eight 80 percent of the time. The good news is that you now have a framework to guide you, when you once only had a guess.

More good news: we're going to spend our time in the rest of this book putting together your personal plan.

But first, there's one more critical stop we have to make.

Scan the QR code to download the My Refill Plan worksheet from my website: refillcoaching.com/my-plan

NOTE

[1] "Quotes," on James Clear's website, https://jamesclear.com/quotes/you-do-not-rise-to-the-level-of-your-goals-you-fall-to-the-level-of-your-systems.

4

The Real Problem

I like having nice tools. I just don't always like having to use them.

Years ago, we bought a house, so I went out and bought a nice lawn mower—not the nicest, but nice for me. I got it at Sears because, back when dinosaurs roamed the earth, Sears was the go-to place for tools, yard equipment, and pretty much everything else you needed to survive in suburbia. It was the OG Walmart. You could get a nice shirt, a Ping-Pong table, and a trailer hitch all under one roof.

I convinced myself to buy a nicer model of mower, with a self-propelled drive and an easy-pull start. *If I buy the nicer mower, I'll be more inclined to mow.*

Flawless logic, or so I thought.

Problem is, I hate mowing. Truth be told, I hate all yard work.

For some, yard work is bliss. They go outside and trim trees, pull weeds, and fix sprinklers to their heart's content. Not me. I like my yard to look nice, but I don't want to be the one to make it look that way. Are you with me? I mean, I'll do it. Grudgingly.

Unenthusiastically. Resentfully. *Why can't the yard mow itself?* But I get it done—mainly because the homeowners association says I have to and I'm too cheap to hire someone to do it for me. I'm not proud of this. I come from a long line of people who love yard work. Somehow, the gene skipped me.

I don't even take good care of the mower. I have never changed the oil, sharpened the blade, or had it tuned up. Honestly, I don't feel bad. It still runs well enough. But it's not in the same kind of shape as when I first bought it. I'm sure it would be a whole lot more effective if I did regular maintenance, but I hate doing maintenance on a mower about as much as I hate mowing with it.

Needless to say, my "buy a great mower, be a great mower" strategy failed. The nicer mower never cured my lack of desire for yard work or yard-machine maintenance. Not even close. I thought having a nice tool would motivate me to do the thing I don't want to do. It didn't. I would mow my lawn, but only often enough to keep the homeowners association off my back and the height of the grass from obscuring my view of the back fence.

How's my grass doing?

I pulled it out and installed artificial turf.

Want to buy a lawn mower? I can hook you up. Cheap.

Systems and Tools Aren't Magic

I'm an enthusiastic proponent of good tools and efficient systems, and I spent the last chapter expounding the virtues of both when it comes to personal replenishment. Simple tools and easy-to-use systems help us solve problems and make progress. They:

- ► Help us get further faster.
- ► Help us stay on track when we wander.
- ► Take a lot of guesswork out of the process and keep us from having to reinvent the wheel.

- ► Produce predictable results.
- ► Give us the ability to make quick adjustments when the results don't match predictions.

But systems and tools aren't magic.

In the same way my lawn mower didn't magically cure my dread of yard work, even good systems won't automatically fix everything when it comes to our stress/replenishment balance.

You've been there, right? You've started the latest fad diet, joined an awesome gym, or bought a cool gadget in hopes that that tool or system would finally solve the problem. You used the same logic I used with the lawn mower—the better/newer/nicer the tool, the greater the motivation and capacity to solve the problem.

But your grass still needs to be cut, right? (Or, to make it more personal, you have laundry hanging on that treadmill in your bedroom.)

Tools and systems must actually be used. They can't solve the problem on their own. Something else needs to be added to the mix.

Tools are good. They aren't God.

In the remaining chapters, we will work on a tool and a system that, if used well, will help you keep burnout away and bring you more health, joy, enthusiasm, and energy. I use this tool, I work this system, and I will help you put it into practice in ways that can change your life.

But before we do that, there's one more thing we need to talk about.

You.

Technical Problems and Adaptive Challenges

Harvard University professors Ronald Heifetz and Marty Linsky changed the way we look at problems. They defined problems in two basic categories: technical problems and adaptive challenges.[1] That framework still guides leaders today. It provides a clear distinction between two types of issues and the different approaches needed to address them.

Technical problems are surface level issues that are relatively simple and straightforward. The solutions to these issues are clear and easy to understand. You only need an expert in the field, a clear set of instructions, or a tool, app, or hack of some kind, and technical problems are easily solved.

Have you ever attempted to put IKEA furniture together? Me too. You go to the big blue warehouse, get a box full of dresser parts, take it home, and dump it out on your living room floor. You grab the instruction manual that looks like it was written by people who don't want you to be able to put furniture together and think, *This would be easy if the instructions were clearer than the hieroglyphics they provided, if they included better tools than the* children's-toy *wrench in the bubble pack, and if there was an instructional video or a* furniture-rookie *hotline to call.* With clear instructions, good tools, and help from an expert, anyone could put furniture together. This is a technical problem.

Adaptive challenges are different. They're more human, nuanced, and complex. The outcome isn't as clear, nor is the fix simple. Solving adaptive challenges requires reexamining attitudes and ingrained actions. People in the middle of the issue will need to do some soul-searching to identify how they have been a contributing factor in the problem. It will require soul-level self-awareness and change.

Conquering adaptive challenges requires development and growth, as opposed to the training and skill building that serves technical problems. A friend of mine says, "You train your dog; you develop your children." Very different approaches to very different issues.

Think of a person you're struggling to lead—maybe it's your senior vice president who can't seem to get his team organized, or maybe it's your fifteen-year-old who can't get his room clean. Which problem do they have? Is it a technical problem—they don't know how to organize and just need some skill building? Or is it more adaptive in nature—they aren't very disciplined and can't bring themselves to do what they need to do when they need to do it?

Remember me buying my lawn mower? I was trying to solve an adaptive issue (I hate yard work) with a technical tool (a nice lawn mower.)

Heifetz and Linsky point out that most problems don't strictly fall into one category. Most issues are a blend of technical and adaptive. Even putting that IKEA dresser together isn't completely technical. I would be more effective at it not only with better tools but with a little bit more patience.

Think of the problems you've tried to conquer in the past, like setting up a fitness program, quitting smoking, getting out of debt, or losing that last ten (or fifty) pounds. What mix of technical and adaptive issues were involved?

If, like me, you've had to figure out a way to lose weight and maintain a healthy lifestyle, you ran into a problem that was both technical and adaptive.

In 2010, I found myself very overweight and beginning to show signs of related health issues. I was an athlete in my younger days. I played high school and college football and knew what it took to take care of my physical health. I knew how to get excess weight off. Most of us do. The technical equation for losing weight is not a mystery—burn more calories than you eat. That's where the technical and adaptive collide. We know how to do it, but it will take some adaptive work to actually do it.

What I needed was not just a new workout strategy and diet but a new mindset and priorities, which are more difficult to adopt than finding the right eating plan and running schedule. I also had to ask different questions: not only, "How can I fit an hour at the gym four days a week into my schedule?" but also, "What are the mental, emotional, and spiritual roadblocks keeping me from doing what I know is needed?"

In my role as a pastor, I've watched many people who were hoping for life transformation run squarely into this issue. They would show up thinking that attending church services, going to Bible studies, and building new relationships would help them overcome lifelong, nagging issues. All of that is helpful, yet what brings transformation is not what happens to a person inside a church building, but it's what happens inside the person as they form a deep, abiding relationship with God and allow inner work to be done.

Are You Your Worst Enemy?

What does this have to do with replenishment?

Only everything.

Human beings have the mysterious ability to do things not in their own best interest. We have the almost inexplicable ability to ignore even our own best advice and do things that will be to our detriment. We can be our own worst enemy.

I am about to help you learn to use a tool and a system to build a plan for your personal replenishment, to replace the guessing and failing that have characterized many of your attempts to pursue personal health and well-being.

But hear me clearly: if you don't address the adaptive challenges that are keeping you from prioritizing your personal replenishment, no plan—not even this one—will help you.

You might want to read that again.

No tool, plan, or clever system will help you without some inner work to uncover and unravel whatever keeps you from prioritizing your personal well-being. If you ignore your adaptive challenges, this tool will eventually become one more treadmill with clothes hanging on it.

The Battle Is Real—and Not Uncommon

What are some of the common adaptive challenges that keep us from prioritizing our personal well-being?

I have looked at myself, my family, my friends, and at people in the very large church I have pastored and have discovered the same challenges coming up time and time again. I have spent the last few years traveling the country speaking to hundreds of business and church leaders, and I shared these challenges to see if they resonated. They did.

Below is a list of what I see as common adaptive challenges:

> Toxic Responsibility
> Chronic Improvement
> Compulsive Achievement
> Hyper-Urgency
> Selective Discipline
> Overserving
> Under-Deserving

I will define each, but first, as you read through the list, are there any that immediately jump out at you? Pay attention to that, because your first instincts may be right.

I also want you to notice two things about these challenges.

First, they are an overuse of your best qualities. If you look at the second word in each descriptor (responsibility, improvement, achievement, and so on), you'd be describing why you got your job and have achieved success. These are your best qualities, your go-to when the pressure is on. They make you comfortable; you'll run in their direction when things hit the fan.

But your best qualities can become your worst enemies when you overuse them to your own detriment. This is where our curious ability to do things that aren't in our own best interests shows up. We become responsible, disciplined, or achievement-oriented to a fault. And that fault can lead us straight to burnout.

The second thing I want you to notice: the ingredient that turns these best qualities into negatives is fear.

Take note of how each one of these adaptive challenges is nothing more than our best qualities mixed with an unhealthy dose of fear:

- ► Add fear to responsibility, and you have toxic responsibility.
- ► Add fear to a sense of urgency, and that good quality that keeps us from complacency and procrastination becomes hyper-urgency and never lets us slow down.
- ► Add fear to a desire to improve things and you get a perfectionist who won't stop working until the project is good enough to make them feel good enough—and it never is.

Fear is a fire. In the right amounts and properly contained, it can keep us alive and safe. Out of control, it will make everything its fuel and burn your house down. Add fear to your best qualities, and you will burn out of control, probably burn yourself out, and maybe even burn those around you.

Look closely at each of these descriptions to find yourself and the adaptive challenge that might be causing you to be your own worst enemy when it comes to taking care of yourself.

Toxic Responsibility

My counselor told me being a responsible person is a good thing; the need to be *the* responsible person is a sickness. Yep. That's me.

Toxic responsibility always needs to keep an eye on everything. It tells you that if you take your eye off the ball for one second, bad things will happen and will be your fault. Toxic responsibility never lets you take a breather, because the minute you turn your back, something under your charge will come off the rails, and you'll be the one to blame.

This is the malady of many chief operating officers and middle managers. It's also common in young parents and new homeowners. They're aware they've been handed a huge responsibility and better not drop the ball. This challenge is often characterized by phantom anxiety—a haunting fear that you're forgetting something you're supposed to have done or that something's coming you should be preparing for but you can't quite remember what it is.

The person with toxic responsibility always needs to be on top of everything but never feels as if they are. They fight their fear of dropping the ball with predictable systems and repeatable processes to minimize the chance anything gets missed. They can be hard on themselves and anyone in their orbit who doesn't appreciate how their well-oiled machine is keeping everything running.

They can't rest or take time to recover because that would mean setting aside their duty to make sure nothing goes wrong. When they do get pried away from their post, they separate themselves far from their responsibilities so no one can accuse them of being irresponsible.

The noble quality of responsibility has become a tyrant keeping them chained to their duties and making them resent the expectations of their job.

Chronic Improvement

Making things better is a fantastic quality. Not being able to stop making things better is perfectionism at its worst.

People who suffer from chronic improvement are never happy with how things are, even if they're really good. They keep honing, tinkering, sharpening, and shaping until they're forced to stop by a deadline or a budget constraint. Sometimes, even those don't stop them.

Chronic improvement whispers that everything can always get better and that it should. Good enough is never good enough. For those who struggle with this adaptive challenge, it's a moral issue. Anyone who leaves anything short of perfection is harshly judged not for their lack of ability but for their lack of care, commitment, or character.

Bosses love having a chronic improver around. They raise the bar of quality for themselves and everyone around them. They don't cut corners or quit before the job is done.

Chronic improvers are not only this way at work. They always have the perfect things in mind for their home and their friends—the perfect meal, the perfect gift, the perfect paint color, the perfect temperature, the perfect beverage, the perfect activity, the perfect look, the perfect experience.

They see how everything can be better with just a little more effort, and they're usually right. The problem isn't that they want to make things better; it's that they don't know how to stop.

This is where burnout sets in for the chronic improver. These helpful and often amazingly creative people will keep improving right past their own time and energy boundaries, which are begging them to stop. They fear if it isn't perfect, it's a poor reflection on them or those they care about. The physical and emotional strain of proving their own worth while making others feel worthy wears them down and can ultimately burn them out.

Compulsive Achievement

Compulsive achievers are most enthusiastic about the mountain in front of them while fairly disinterested in talking about the mountain behind. That was the past. You can't rest on your laurels.

Why look back when there's so much ahead? Been there, done that, got the T-shirt to prove it—now let's get on with what's next!

They may not even be finished climbing one mountain when they spot the next and start gearing up to conquer it. It's exciting for the compulsive achiever but terribly discouraging to the people who signed up for the first expedition. That's why the compulsive achiever is as good at burning out those around them as they are at burning themselves out. Even though they have a lot of hardware in their trophy cases, they don't celebrate well because, frankly, they just don't have time for it. When the team is hoping there will be a party to acknowledge what they accomplished, the chronic achiever is worried the past achievement might make everyone complacent to the point they'll never climb again. That's their driving fear. Because achievement is their drug of choice, they fear every accomplishment might be their last.

Don't get me wrong—their successes aren't just for show. They are doing significant things. They feel called. They're moving with intention. What they accomplish will change the world in meaningful ways. It's not a game for them, but it's still addicting.

Much like chronic improvement, the problem with compulsive achievers isn't that they are doing important work; they just can't stop doing it long enough to rest. Eventually, their tank runs dry.

Anyone with a sense of adventure loves following the compulsive achiever. There's never a dull moment, as they're constantly achieving new and important things and have an incredible vision for what's next.

But without the ability to stop, celebrate, recover, and restock the supplies, their expedition could come to a painful, screeching halt.

Hyper-Urgency

The hyper-urgent have that look in their eyes. They've got to go—now. They always have something on fire that needs immediate attention. They're a little curious about why you're not moving faster, too. If you're in front of them in traffic, you might get the horn half a second after the light turns green. If you're trying to follow them somewhere, be prepared to keep up.

If you know this person, you're pretty sure he or she is going to burn out at some point, probably soon.

We love having them around in a crisis, though. They aren't phased by the elevated stress created by the seriousness of a situation. They jump in, move quickly, accomplish a lot, and even seem energized by the adrenaline. They have sharp, quick minds that work well when the heat is on. But when the adrenaline wears off, they can sink into a funk. They don't do well for long when there's nothing requiring their gift for handling an emergency. When the hyper-urgent are handling a crisis (or even running an everyday project), they can make everyone around them feel like they're moving too slowly or not doing enough.

The "hyper" part of their urgency makes it sound like they're frantic, but these people usually aren't panicky. They are just clear about what needs to happen and certain that wasting time is bad.

The hyper-urgent are typically very efficient and don't make many mistakes. That's not to say they never make mistakes. The part of their urgency pushing them to go faster can cause speed wobble when they get tired.

They often deplete their energy quickly because of how much fuel their intensity burns. They usually recover quickly but can burn themselves out so suddenly and thoroughly that quick recovery is no longer an option.

Selective Discipline

If you've ever wondered why you're diligent and methodical in many parts of your life but have a glaring area that is undisciplined and unfocused, this is it.

Selective discipline is a lot like selective listening (which I am accused of on a regular basis.) It picks and chooses what things will receive the best of your attention and effort, and it leaves other things unattended.

If you looked at my desk where I'm currently sitting, you would see that it's fairly orderly. Papers and files are in folders or binders, or at least in tidy stacks where I can get at them quickly. I know exactly what's in each and could easily get my hands on anything you asked me for.

The workbench in the garage is another story entirely.

There is a lot of stuff on it. A lot. I'm not exactly sure what it all is, but I'm sure I need it for something. If you asked me if you could borrow some epoxy, a hacksaw, a wire nut, or ceiling fan bracket, I'm sure they're in there. But you're going to have to wait as I dig through the heaping pile of stuff that looks like a toddler organized it (no offense to toddlers). I'm disciplined, just not with that.

That's how selective discipline works. If this is you, you've been baffled at how you can run a business, manage a family, and oversee a budget yet not be able to consistently eat healthily, maintain spiritual practices, or remember your kid's baseball schedule. No one would accuse you of not being disciplined, yet there are areas of your life in which you haven't found a way to apply that same level of structure. It's not an ability thing. It's not a character thing. It's a block. There's a reason.

For the selectively disciplined, a choice has been made about what is important and what's not—about what they can get by with and what will cost them in ways that matter to them. In some ways, they are conserving energy for what really matters. Oftentimes, the selectively disciplined will give themself permission to let things go by saying something like, "Because I'm so disciplined in *this* area of my life, I can afford to let this *other* area go." We all do this. But the fallout from this kind of selection process happens when things that do matter or will matter get treated like they don't or won't.

Personal replenishment and well-being practices often, very often, get left on the back burner and receive minimal attention, even from those who live remarkably disciplined lives. It's only after years that their inattentiveness to healthy habits and rhythms show up as burnout. Those who witness it say the same thing as the person who crashed: "I never saw it coming." Read back through my story at the beginning of this book, and you'll hear me say that.

People who struggle with this assume it's the easiest of the adaptive challenges to overcome. They believe the answer is simply to apply more discipline, but what's actually needed is a change of priorities.

Overserving

Have you ever been overserved? Maybe you've eaten at a restaurant where the waiter would not go away. They stopped by the table every couple of minutes to check on you. They had way too many suggestions about what you should order. They engaged you in conversation about things no one at the table wanted to talk about. They refilled your iced tea after you just got the right amount of sugar mixed in. They took your plate before you were done. It's nice that they were attentive, but too much of a good thing was still too much.

Have you ever been tempted to be an over-server?

If so, it's part of why we love you. You are the kind of person who has the twin superpowers of thoughtfulness and kindness. You see the needs around you and move to respond almost immediately. More than that, you can anticipate what will be needed and plan to have resources available no one else thought to provide.

Your friends and colleagues think you are amazing. You're almost magic in the way you can pull a rabbit out of your hat the minute someone suggests that everything would be better if we just had a rabbit. You are the go-to person in your office, neighborhood, kid's school, or sports team.

You often say to yourself, "You take care of everyone else; when are you going to make some time to take care of you?" That's where your burnout begins.

The over-server is the cousin of the toxically responsible. They feel their need to serve others as a moral imperative. Over-servers aren't usually looking for credit or attention; being helpful is in the fabric of their identity and character. Because of this, getting the over-server to commit to personal replenishment requires a change of conviction. Serving themselves feels so wrong, but it's the only way they'll be able to use their best quality for the long haul.

Under-Deserving

Of these adaptive challenges, this one is not like the others in that the term describes a negative. It points to the shadow side of all the challenges and a mindset that causes many to feel undeserving of investing in themselves.

I could have called this excessive humility, although I'm just not sure there's such a thing as too much humility. But this challenge does look on the outside like the overuse of the positive quality of meekness. In reality, it's not. It is more akin to insecurity than true humility.

Under-deservers don't think of themselves as worthy of the kind of self-care they need. They believe their personal well-being is not that big a deal. If you ask how they're doing, they'll most likely tell you they're fine. They won't tell you about their successes or problems either. They really don't want to talk that much about themselves at all. They are happy to discuss the projects they're working on, people they are serving, or current events; they just don't talk about themselves.

Usually, this challenge of feeling undeserving of personal care is a ride-along issue accompanying another one. It shows up as a secondary challenge attached to a more primary adaptive issue. For instance, the toxically responsible might feel their important role of taking care of the organization is a much higher priority than taking care of themselves. They don't see themselves as deserving of effort and attention. Or the hyper-urgent don't see the need for self-care as critical as the fires they're fighting. Feeling undeserving is most commonly paired with overserving, looking for ways to help others rather than spending any time considering how they might need to refill their own depleted tank.

In Deep

This list of adaptive challenges certainly isn't exhaustive, but it can help you identify which challenge or two are pushing back on your need for regular habits and rhythms that prioritize your well-being.

As you begin to unpack and unravel your own challenges, I want to give you this caveat: They won't go away easily. They may never go away.

You should get some help working through these issues. You might even need a counselor. Just be warned: even when you do all that, they will still be with you, at least to some degree.

Why?

Fear doesn't give up easily.

When I went to my counselor to understand my own burnout, toxic responsibility came quickly to the surface. I began to understand why it was there—my natural temperament, upbringing, etc. But why was it so strong? Why did it push me so hard? Why did it never let me rest? Why was I willing to blow past any boundary of healthy work hours and ignore the opportunities for soul care offered to me? Why was the fear so unrelenting?

There was a reason.

In counseling, I found it.

A year or so after our family moved to Las Vegas, we took our three young boys to a friend's house, where several families and a lot of kids gathered to play, eat, and swim. As the afternoon wore on and parents grew tired of wrangling kids around the yard, we decided to herd the kids into a room with a big television so they could watch a movie and the parents could recover.

I made sure our kids were safely in the room, particularly because our oldest son, Adam, who was four years old and very curious, tended to wander when told to stay put. When I was sure he was settled in, I found a comfortable place to sit, and I eventually started to nod off for a nap.

Then something told me to get up and check on Adam one more time. I dragged myself away from the nap and headed into the movie room to count heads, especially Adam's. He was gone.

You know the first place I went.

I sprinted into the backyard. *Please God, not the pool.* I ran across the patio and around the corner of the house to find my son about eighteen inches under water—still conscious—reaching up for the surface of the pool. I got to him, grabbed his outstretched arm, and pulled him out of the water. He had already started turning blue. He took a big breath of air, which I promptly hugged right back out of him. He was scared but fine. I was shaken—more than I knew at the time.

The thought that kept running through my head in the hours and even years after? *If I had been ninety seconds less responsible, our son would be gone.*

Did you hear that? *Less responsible.* In that moment and in several others like it throughout my life, I identified that my natural temperament of being a responsible person became the adaptive challenge of toxic responsibility. I have carried it with me ever since. Fear holds on tight.

This is so important because these challenges, with their accompanying fear, will talk you out of prioritizing your personal well-being. Mine says, "If you don't keep your eyes on everything, if you're not relentlessly responsible, catastrophically bad things will happen, and they will be your fault." What do you think that has done to my ability to take a day off or a real vacation?

Your adaptive challenges might also be that deep in you. They hold on tight and whisper in your ear, trying to talk you out of things you should be talking yourself into. What have your challenges been telling you lately about taking time for yourself? They will probably never stop doing that. We've just got to be ready to push back.

Sign up for a session with a counselor. Talk to your pastor. Confide in a friend. Share it with your business partner. Let someone know the struggle you have in prioritizing the things you know are good for you. Give them permission to ask you tough questions.

Don't let these challenges talk you out of building and using the replenishment plan that just might change your life.

NOTE

[1]Ronald A. Heifetz, Marty Linsky, and Alexander Grashow, *The Practice of Adaptive Leadership: Tools and Tactics for Changing Your Organization and the World* (Harvard Business Press, 2009).

5

The Plan—Begin with Rest

Are you ready?

It's time to start building the plan that will keep your tank full. Ultimately, your plan will feature five key habits.[1]

While each habit is helpful on its own, greater benefit comes when you put them together in a personalized plan that guides you into regular rhythms of replenishment.

We begin with rest, and snipe hunting.

Snipe Hunting 101

Ever been on a snipe hunt?

These days, sniping is what you do to snag that deal from eBay, swooping in at the last millisecond with your winning bid, but that's not the snipe hunt I remember.

Snipe hunts usually happened on Boy Scout camping trips, where the newbies would be led into the woods with bags and told to hide in a bush, snowdrift, or other really terrible place. They were to wait for everyone else (the in-group) to chase the illusive (imaginary) snipe in their direction. There were usually elaborate descriptions of what snipes looked like, how fast they ran, and how difficult they were to catch. Equal to the flowery description of the snipe was the enthusiastic explanation of how much fun the hunt would be and how the best spot on the snipe-hunting team was the bag holder. "You really want to be the one holding the bag," they said. "It'll be great!" Yeah, right.

These friends (torturers) promised that if you waited long enough, were really quiet, held the bag just right, and didn't leave your post no matter how cold it was or who you heard laughing in the distance, eventually, a snipe would come along.

If you were one of the newbies, you would soon find yourself sitting in misery for what seemed like hours with an empty bag and no sign of either snipes or the in-group. Welcome to the snipe hunt.

You'd finally figure out there were no such things as snipes, and you had trusted the wrong people.

What you were waiting for was never going to show.

Finding rest can be a little like that.

Rest

"You need to take a couple of days and get some rest."

Ever had anyone tell you that? Sounds promising, right? Unless you are no longer a newbie. If you've been around the block a few times, it sounds a bit like, "Let's go on a snipe hunt."

I talk with so many people who struggle to identify what getting rest looks like for them. Either it's been so long since anything felt restful, or they've never reflected enough to discern what rest feels like for them.

In a culture that values productivity and speed, the ability to rest has atrophied. The Centers for Disease Control and

Prevention reported that in 2022, one out of every three adults in the United States was not getting enough sleep.[2]

Let's start with this question: What is restful to you?

Don't rush past that. Take at least two minutes on it. Find a blank page in the back of this book or in your journal, and start making a list; then add to it as you become aware of what gives you rest.

Think back to a time when you found yourself refreshed, renewed, and energized. You felt like you had fuel in the tank, breath in your lungs, the capacity to handle whatever was ahead of you. What caused that? What did you do that made you feel that way?

Perhaps you spent time in a relaxing location with a fruity drink and zero responsibilities. Or maybe you took a wild trip down a class five rapids and ran a half-marathon through a National Park.

Getting rest looks different for everyone. What is restful to me might drain you. You may know this from the trip to the beach you took with your spouse. They were completely content to lounge on the beach all day with a good book. You were losing your mind: *How can anyone sit still for that long?* They were annoyed with you for not being able to relax. You were annoyed with them for wasting a perfectly good day doing nothing.

As I was unpacking this concept with a group of business leaders, one started talking wistfully about his love of yard work. He waxed eloquent about how he enjoyed spending a day pushing his mower around the yard, grooming his planter boxes, and trimming his trees. For a moment, he was transported. His whole countenance changed as he went on and on about how relaxing it was to get lost in a day of landscape maintenance.

I was dying inside. I've mentioned my disdain for yard work. They call it yard *work* for a reason. The last thing I want to do when I'm fatigued is the first thing he wants to do to find rest. The two of us couldn't be more different. More accurately, we couldn't be more unique.

And so are you.

What helps you to rest? What are you doing when you're truly resting?

Go ahead. Get started on that list. We'll come back to it.

Not Working

Whatever you're doing when you're resting, I guarantee you are not doing this:

Working.

Resting is what you're doing when you're not working. This doesn't just mean you've left the office or stopped doing chores around the house. It means you have ceased whatever activity feels like work to you and started recovering from the depletion that work caused.

Parents of young children have a difficult time finding moments when they're not working because when they come home from their job, there's still work to do. Executives and managers exit the office only to head home to bills that need paying and a spare bedroom that needs painting. Even though they're not at work, they're still working. It's only when they stop doing whatever feels like work that rest can truly begin.

Think of it like this: Muscles in a resting state are not under the tension that comes from doing their work. When they're in this state, we say they are at rest. When you stop whatever is work to you, you're at rest too.

One obstacle to finding rest is our inability to draw a clear line between working and not working. Cell phones and other technologies have erased the lines we used to draw between working and resting. Every notification from our phones, laptops, tablets, and now even refrigerators, vehicles, and watches demands we spring into action. When they ding, flash, or vibrate, we obediently go to work to respond to whatever they're telling us requires our attention and effort.

I'm not here to bash technology. I am currently writing this on my laptop, I have a smartwatch on my wrist that's connected to my cell phone, and my watch vibrates to tell me I have a text or email. My phone is connected to my laptop so I can see texts and emails when they arrive without looking at my phone. In fairness, I am working right now, and there's nothing wrong with work.

The question is: Can we stop working when it's time to stop?

A car that won't start is a problem. A car that won't stop can be deadly. You know how to start working. The real question is, *Do you know how to stop?*

Remember the scene that played during the opening credits of every episode of *The Flintstones*? Fred is out working at the rock quarry on a brontosaurus. His supervisor checks his sundial watch, sees that it's quitting time, and pulls a bird's tail. The bird squawks, telling Fred it's time to stop working. With a big "yabba dabba doo!" Fred slides down off the brontosaurus, lands in his car, and heads home to get Wilma, Pebbles, and Dino, their pet dinosaur. They pick up Barney, Betty, and Bam Bam, and all head to the drive-in for a movie.

Fred had a clear signal that let him know when it was time to stop working. There was a distinct line between work and not working.

We have erased that line. Or at least we have blurred it almost to oblivion.

A problem with maintaining that line today is that the hardest work to shut off is the work we do with our minds, not with our hands. We are constantly problem-solving, worrying, writing imaginary emails, and having future conversations in our mind. Even those who work in positions primarily characterized by physical labor and who have a clear start and stop to their workday still struggle to shut their minds off at night and on weekends. Executives and homemakers alike struggle to shut off the work going on between their ears, even when the office is closed or the kids are in bed. Even though we might be away from our formal workplaces, we feel like we've got to keep managing responsibilities, formulating improvements, or strategizing our next achievement. We can't shut it off.

This is what keeps us from resting when we're not at work and makes rest so elusive. Turns out, not working takes a little work.

As we build a plan to balance stress and replenishment, we begin by identifying blocks of time when we will cease from our work.

No-Work Zones

You need some well-placed no-work zones.

Before you panic, I'm not talking about sitting for hours staring at a wall—unless staring at a wall is helpful. If it is, find a nice wall and knock yourself out.

You need to identify periods of time in the framework of your daily, weekly, monthly, periodic (every three to four months), and annual rhythms when you stop working. Using the tool found on page 58, ask yourself, "When will I not work?"

Specific, recurring periods of rest are nothing new. For millennia, major religions have set aside Sabbaths meant to allow people, animals, and even farmland to rest. Probably the most recognizable of these is the Judeo-Christian practice of a weekly Sabbath day, a twenty-four-hour period set aside for rest, reflection, and worship. It was established during the exodus of Israel from captivity in Egypt. As the Israelites crossed the desert, God gave them this instruction: "This is what the Lord commanded: Tomorrow will be a day of complete rest, a holy Sabbath day set apart for the Lord" (Exod. 16:23 NLT).

Later, as the Levitical law was established to help govern the new nation of Israel, this was written into their code: "You have six days each week for your ordinary work, but the seventh day is a Sabbath day of complete rest, an official day for holy assembly. It is the LORD's Sabbath day, and it must be observed wherever you live" (Lev. 23:3 NLT).

Although there are devout people who still observe days like these, our 24/7 culture can make consistent downtime feel archaic and obsolete.

It's not.

You need this, and you know it.

Identifying these periods of rest does two things.

First, they signal that you need to shut off your work. Just like with Fred Flintstone, something happens when we have a signal that says work now stops. Clearly defined no-work zones keep work from filling every available space in our schedule and attention. Having these boundaries allows us to keep work in its place.

I have a go-to phrase I use when I find work trying to creep into my no-work zone. I declare, "I don't have to do that right now," and I picture the time on my calendar I've identified for doing my work. It helps me remember I have adequate time to do this work so I don't have to worry about doing it now.

The second thing no-work zones do is give you the opportunity to practice the internal skill of choosing to be present. When you step across the line from work zone to no-work zone, you know it's time to be present—home with family, connecting with friends, focusing on your workout, enjoying your favorite hobby.

As I was helping a friend with this concept, I asked if he had an identifiable time when work ceased for him every day. He didn't. My friend runs a successful company in a very challenging industry. He also has a wife and two teenage boys he adores. Like many, he's struggled with finding a way to stop thinking about work so he can be fully present with his family when he gets home. I suggested using his after-work commute—a drive of about forty minutes—to decompress, let his mind debrief his workday, and prep for anything he needs tomorrow. I asked if something could help signal him to stop his internal work-related debrief/prep. He decided when the front tires of his truck hit the gravel driveway leading to his house, it would be his signal to put work away and be present with his family.

Setting up no-work zones makes space so you can become skilled at resting.

One important note: as you're setting up your replenishment plan, resist the temptation to put your restful activities in the "rest" column. Here's why: the "rest" column should be reserved only for identifying the no-work zones. For instance, my current plan has some no-work time blocked on Saturday morning (from the time I wake up until noon), Saturday evening (from 6 p.m. until bedtime), Sunday evening, and other times blocked out on a weekly basis. It looks like this:

	REST
DAILY	Sleep = 10 p.m.–6 a.m. Work = 9 hours (Done: 9 p.m.)
WEEKLY	Sat. morning Sat. evening Sun. afternoon/evening Mon. morning Mon. evening
MONTHLY	Day Away—7 hrs — Change Scenery LLV — Clean Out 9–Noon — Clear Space Patio/Fire pit
PERIODICALLY	Get Away Days 3–4 days/3–4 mo Add on to Travel Alaska?
ANNUALY	Summer Vacation — 10 Days

Later, as we talk about the other rhythms (release, recreate, relate, etc.), those activities will naturally find their way into the no-work zones we're identifying now.

Here are some ideas about how the no-work zones might show up in daily, weekly, monthly, periodic, and annual rhythms.

Daily

Daily no-work zones focus primarily on the routines of sleep and work.

The easiest place to start is setting aside your sleep hours. What hours will you block out for sleep?

I have identified 10 p.m. to 6 a.m. as my sleep time. I use 10 p.m. as a marker to put away any residual work I may be doing and start slowing myself down toward rest. When that time shows up, I turn the temperature down a click or two, start turning the lights off, and head into other evening rituals that remind me the day is over and it's time to sleep. I typically drift off to sleep by 10:30 p.m. and wake up between 5:00 and 5:30 a.m.—usually without an alarm.

Many people ask what I believe is the optimum number of hours of sleep you should get. My answer? How many hours of sleep do you need to be at an eight 80 percent of the time? I've had people tell me they can get by on four hours of sleep. That's fine. I can, too. But I can't do that for very long and still show up at an eight 80 percent of the time.

Setting up consistent sleep hours does for you the two things we just talked about: it gives you a signal that it's time to shut off work, and it helps you build the skill of only doing what you're doing during that time—which in this case is sleeping.

Here are some other daily no-work routines to consider:

- ► Dinner and family time: no phones at the table, no lap-tops from 6 p.m. to 8 p.m., etc.
- ► Morning quiet time: no phones, television, or technology. Use this time for prayer, reflection, meditation, conversation with spouse or roommates, etc.
- ► Lunch breaks: claim this time during your workday to rest.
- ► Set work hours: limit your daily work hours by asking, "How many hours of work can I do and still be at an eight 80 percent of the time?"

Weekly

Creating bigger blocks of time every week allows for rhythms that refresh you.

Remember when we all took a day off? From the time you woke up until the time you went to sleep, you were able to do things that refreshed you and restored you. Days like these are still needed for us to show up at our best when it's time to work.

Taking an entire day off each week may seem impossible, but identifying blocks of time as no-work zones will serve you well. Ask, "What significant blocks of time can become rhythms of rest each week?" Again, these are not activities, but they are periods of time during which you can do restorative activities.

Weekly no-work zones for me include Saturday morning until noon and Sunday afternoon through Monday at noon. Because part of my life's work has centered around serving churches, I have developed the rhythm of seeing Sunday afternoon as my "finish line" for the week. Once the worship services are complete, I'm done. Sunday afternoon, Sunday evening, and Monday morning have become a significant period of rest and recovery that let me intentionally shut work down and lean into recovery. As my consulting work with businesses and business leaders has increased, that Sunday finish line and the time of rest that follows it have remained a critical piece of my weekly rhythms.

Here are some questions to help identify your weekly no-work zones:

- ▶ When is your weekly finish line?
- ▶ What day makes the most sense for a significant period of downtime?
- ▶ When can you schedule household work (paying bills, cleaning, mowing, etc.) so you can prioritize a significant block of down time?
- ▶ Where could you clean up "slop time" (work slopping over into potentially useful down time)?

Monthly

Making time each month to reset and recalibrate pays you back in both perspective and speed.

Taking time every thirty days to pause and recover allows you to take a deeper breath than you're able to weekly.

I take one day a month away from my office and my weekly routines to practice what I call my "day away." To rest more deeply and make the day intentionally different, I change the scenery by driving forty-five minutes across town from where I live in Las Vegas to a resort community with a lake. It's just enough of a shift from my norm to let me leave daily and weekly stresses and find a different perspective. I use the day to make space for practices that help me reflect on and recover from a month's worth of challenges. It's an opportunity for me to think more freely and reflect more deeply. I talk to God and listen to him a little longer. I look a bit farther down the road than I can in the hustle of a week.

A day like this is just one type of monthly practice that can help you recover and reset. You might take an afternoon off once a month to spend with family, you might go on a hike, or you might catch up on all the books and articles you've been meaning to get to.

When could you block out a significant amount of time every month to help you show up at your best?

Periodically

Longer breaks every three to four months are like a bye week in the schedule of a football team. They allow you to heal and regain strength in ways that aren't possible in shorter breaks.

When you pound in nails, every strike begins with the hammer being drawn back to gather potential energy. A rhythm is set—draw back, strike, draw back, strike—until the nail is pounded into the wood. That illustrates how daily and weekly rhythms work. Monthly rhythms of rest are like a carpenter stopping to align the next piece of wood so it can be nailed into place. A periodic break is like a carpenter sitting down for a minute to catch his breath, get a drink of water, and come back ready to put up the next wall.

Periodic breaks take preparation and investment. They should be strategically placed as part of the recovery phase of a season of work. Accountants would do well to place a periodic break in May as they recover from the rush of tax season. Pastors might plan a break like this after the Christmas season or Easter services. School teachers can use their semester schedules or school holidays to plan meaningful four- or five-day breaks. The key is to recognize your patterns of work stress throughout the year and plan to meet them with periodic breaks that refill and renew. Finding the right time and place to spend these breaks will determine how effective they will be. You will have to invest time and potentially finances to plan and execute these kinds of breaks, but the price you pay will be more than worth it.

Here are some questions to help you identify periodic breaks from your work:

- ► What are the seasonal stress patterns of your work?
- ► When would you feel the most relief from a long weekend away?
- ► What locations could become your go-to places for periodic breaks?
- ► How far in advance do you need to plan this type of getaway?

Annually

Longer breaks every year do more for you than you might imagine. You will make memories with family or friends that should be more than enough to make you prioritize this kind of extended time off. The added benefit of an annual vacation is the way it confronts your adaptive challenge and gives you an opportunity to grow personally.

The idea of a vacation is that you vacate your work for a while so you can fully recover. Ask yourself, *How long does my vacation need to be for me to recover my energy and return to work with a full tank? How long do I need to be away for a vacation to do what it's meant to do?*

These longer annual breaks do for us what none of the other lengths of time off for rest do. They make us wrestle with our identity. Who are you if you're not working? Who are you away from your title, office, position, or even your home? Who are you without your laptop or access to your company email? You'll find out on a good, long break.

Like periodic breaks, the best annual breaks take planning and investment. You'll need to coordinate your calendar, delegate decision-making authority (not just tasks), make a financial plan, and determine day-to-day logistics at work and at home. (Who's going to open the shop? Who's going to watch the dog?)

There's one more critical component to getting rest.

Rest and Trust

I can't sleep in the car when someone else is driving.

The reason I can't is because, well, someone else is driving.

Every bump, jerk, lane change, or speed adjustment means we're driving off the road or heading for a collision. If I had confidence that whoever was driving was as competent behind the wheel as I am, it might be a different story.

But I don't, so I keep driving. Then I get tired and find myself falling asleep at the wheel.

The problem is, I've never found anyone I trust to drive like me.

The same lack of trust contributed to my burnout.

If you want to set aside your work to find rest, you'll have to wrestle with this question: *Who would I have to trust so I could let go of the wheel long enough to get the rest I need?* If you're sensing that's both a practical and a spiritual question, you're right.

The relationship between trust and rest presents a practical question: Who are the right people for you to hand responsibility to so you can create no-work zones for yourself? If you don't find these people and actually trust them to "drive the car," your toxic responsibility or compulsive achievement will run unchecked and will never let you set aside work so you can rest. Putting your work in the hands of good people and then looking them in the eye as you tell them you trust them frees you to rest and empowers them to bring their best.

This only works when we understand that trust is first a choice we make before it's a feeling we experience. Choose to trust, and you'll eventually get to rest in that trust. Withhold trust, and it will keep you up at night.

The relationship between trust and rest also has a spiritual component. When you consider who you'd have to trust to find real, soul-deep rest, your beliefs come into the picture.

I follow and trust Jesus, so the issue should be decided. My faith in him should allow me to rest without concern for what tomorrow will hold. Sadly, I still wrestle with the depth of my trust in God, and it shows in the level at which I'm able to rest. The more I trust God, the more I find rest.

Jesus pointed out this relationship between rest and trust:

> Then Jesus said, "Come to me, all of you who are weary and carry heavy burdens, and I will give you rest. Take my yoke upon you. Let me teach you, because I am humble and gentle at heart, and you will find rest for your souls. For my yoke is easy to bear, and the burden I give you is light." (Matt. 11:28–30 NLT)

Jesus indicates that he has a version of rest that comes when we bring our burdens to him and take on his approach to life.

I've noticed my adaptive challenges place the enormously heavy burden of producing success, making progress, meeting expectations, and avoiding failure squarely on my shoulders. My yoke is heavy. Really heavy. What Jesus offers is a not only a new approach that is lighter but that also includes help—his help—in carrying it.

My adaptive challenges tell me I'm required to know everything, to own every outcome, and to do everything to make those outcomes happen. That yoke burned me out.

These days, I'm learning that God knows everything. I don't know what's going to happen twenty minutes from now, and neither do you. But he does. So I'll trust him.

My faith tells me God is in charge of the outcomes. A farmer friend of mine explained crop failure to me. He said it's what happens when you do everything right and then realize you're not in charge of the weather. There are no guaranteed outcomes. Only someone outside of our world can guarantee what will happen inside it. Again, I'm learning to trust.

I'm also realizing God is always at work. I live in a system of limits—to my time, energy, resources. I can't always be on the job. I have to sleep sometime, and so do you. But if God is qualified to be God, he doesn't require rest in the way I do. He's never not on the job. That helps me let him run the world while I get some rest.

If you aren't a spiritual person, I'm not asking you to adopt my approach. I respect your choice and ability to filter what isn't in your worldview. But still, whether you are a religious person or not, I hope you don't miss the principle: the more you trust, the more you can rest.

Let someone else take the wheel for a while, and go get some sleep.

NOTES

[1] It will be helpful to refer to the worksheet on page 58 as we navigate through each of these habits.

[2] "FastStats: Sleep in Adults," CDC, accessed May 2, 2025, https://www.cdc.gov/sleep/data-research/facts-stats/adults-sleep-facts-and-stats.html.

6

Release

You never know what will end up in your backpack.

I saw a video of some friends who found a beach at the bottom of a steep cliff. They climbed down the three hundred or so stairs graciously provided to get to the ocean so they could go for a swim.

While one of the guys was out swimming, his buddy took the liberty of filling the bottom of his backpack with rocks and then stuffing clothes on top of them so they would go unnoticed—at least for a while.

When the friends finished swimming, they grabbed their stuff and headed back up the massive flight of stairs. The unsuspecting backpack carrier was doing okay for a little while but eventually started to struggle under the weight of the pack full of rocks. At first, he only made a few comments about how steep the stairs were and how he must just be tired. The more he climbed, the more his complaints turned into expletive-filled rants about how tough it was to keep going and how weak he must be.

It didn't help that his friends were enjoying his struggle a little too much. It was all in fun, but as I watched, it felt familiar, how the very people responsible for his heavy load were the ones chiding him for not being able to carry it.

When they got to the top of the stairs, Backpack Guy was thoroughly worn out and cussing more than ever. The rocks had done their job, but the fun wasn't over.

When he looked up, he noticed the road that led to where they parked the car was a steady climb up another hill. He was done.

He cussed a bit more and flung the backpack off. When it hit the ground, it landed with an unfamiliar thud. *What the . . .?!*

He started unpacking the contents and found the rocks his so-called friends had left for him.

He had a good laugh about it. They had a great laugh about it.

He cussed a lot more. He told his friends how much he hated them.

They all laughed together.

And I gained a great opening for this chapter.

The Weight

We all carry rocks.

They end up in our backpacks, and we take them with us up the hills and through the valleys of life. They weigh us down and wear us out.

They are given to us along the way. Some are small. We tell ourselves they're no big deal and to just keep carrying them. After all, we're strong and can take it, right? Others are huge and heavy and demand we make adjustments so they don't crush us.

If we end up carrying enough, it becomes difficult to carry anything else.

These rocks are the emotionally heavy experiences that happen to us and add weight to our load. Whether it's the heaviness of leadership or of life, there is no shortage of situations that create emotional weight. Stuff happens, things break, mistakes are made, loved ones get sick, rent goes up, people make (stupid) choices, criticisms come, life changes, drama ensues, pressure mounts, and all of it adds to the load we carry.

Let's be clear: it's not what happens, but it's the emotions that come with it that feel so heavy. It's the grief following the loss of a loved one, or your disappointment in a friend, or the angst accompanying your kid's choice of college (or no college), or the anxiety preceding the difficult conversation you're about to have with the slacker employee. That's the heaviness you feel. Because of this, it's essential we understand our emotions and how they affect us. Fortunately, there are a lot of people to offer help.

Core Emotions

In 1987, professor Peter Salovey (who went on to become the president of Yale University) had his friend, professor John Mayer, come over to help him with some painting around his house. The conversation they had as they worked together that day would become the genesis of a theory that would describe intelligence in a new way: emotional intelligence.[1] The research and books that followed have helped many to not only identify their emotions but develop competencies to access them as they relate to the world and others. The studies around emotional intelligence have produced a list of core emotions, which help us better understand what's going on inside us.

Paul Eckman, professor emeritus of psychology at the University of California, San Francisco, has also led the charge to understand our emotions more deeply. In a cool, pop-culture twist, he was approached by Pete Docter from Pixar Animation Studios to be the scientific consultant on the 2015 movie *Inside Out*, which follows the journey of a little girl dealing with her core emotions.[2]

He also made a list of core emotions that humans have. The lists from these studies are, not surprisingly, very similar. They group our core emotions into six categories: joy/happiness, surprise, sadness, fear, anger, and disgust.

Joy/Happiness

This is the primary emotion in that it's the one we all want. It's not the superficial giddiness of a child getting a new toy. Rather, it's a deep and abiding satisfaction with life. When parents are asked, "What do you want for your kids?" they reply like all parents: "I want my kids to be happy."

Joy energizes and lifts us. It's the emotion that makes life lighter. Joy is what we experience when we can say, "This is good, and more good is coming."

We can also experience joy when things aren't going well. In those circumstances, we can experience joy when we can say, "This isn't good, but good is coming."

Joy puts wind in our sails and fuel in our tank. It is essential to life. In *Inside Out*, when the main character, Joy, gets lost, the whole system (the inner world of the young girl) starts shutting down. That's pretty instructive about the way we work.

Surprise

Surprise is a neutral emotion. Some have called it a gateway emotion. Surprise produces the feelings consistent with whatever the surprise is. If someone told you, "Surprise! You just won the lottery!" you'd have one kind of emotion. If they said, "Surprise! Your house just burned down," you'd have a very different feeling.

Surprise and joy are the two emotions that have the potential of lightening our emotional load. The other four core emotions are where the weight comes from.

Sadness

This is the feeling we get when we lose something we value. It doesn't really matter what it is—it just matters that it matters to us. When someone dear to us dies, or if we move and lose the daily contact we once enjoyed, grief shows up as a painful indicator of how much we love them. We can even feel the weight of grief when a season of life or work we deeply enjoyed fades away or hopes and dreams don't materialize. If sadness becomes pervasive enough, it can turn to depression and despair.

Fear

For most of us, fear is easy to identify. The butterflies in our stomach, knots in our throats, sweat on our brows, and the pounding heart in our chest let us know when fear has come to visit.

Fear is the anticipation that something of value is going to be lost. We feel it most when our sense of safety is lost. A close second might be when our sense of personal significance and value are threatened.

Fear doesn't have a very sophisticated regulator. It usually comes in hot, takes no prisoners, and won't leave until it's sure everything's okay. Fear is trying to tell us as clearly as possible that safety is the top priority. To make sure it has our attention, it usually grabs us by the throat and hangs on tight, despite any attempt to reason with it. Fear will make us do things our rational mind would never let us get away with. Fear might not always be clear about why it showed up, but it will not be ignored.

As much as we'd like to live fearlessly, we need fear to function as our early warning system for threats to our well-being.

Anger

Like fear, anger tries to get our attention. It wants us—and everyone around us—to know that someone or something is getting in the way of what matters deeply to us. This is why it often shows up when a loved one passes away. We're sad for the loss, but we're mad at whatever caused it. Anger is the white-hot reaction that shoots daggers of emotion at anything that keeps us from what we want. And the more we want it, the more anger we feel when our attempts to get it are thwarted.

Anger comes on strong and actually makes us physically stronger in an attempt to help us conquer whatever obstacle is in between us and what we desire. Because of this, anger is a danger. It's like fire. When it's contained and under control, it can be a useful tool. A righteous sense that things aren't as they should be has started hospitals, initiated humanitarian movements, and built churches. But when anger gets out of control—and let's be honest, it's a pretty volatile substance to start with—it can burn relationships to the ground. It is highly combustible and can turn a little spark into a forest fire, consuming the landscape quickly.

Disgust

You can almost feel this emotion just by saying its name. It sounds like you're hacking something up out of your throat and spitting it out of your mouth, and that's what disgust does.

Disgust is your repugnance meter. It tells you when you want nothing to do with the things coming your way. Disgust pulls the emotional rip cord and says, "I'm out. I'm done." The phrase that often goes with this emotion is, "I can't stand it anymore." Disgust tells us when our tolerance has reached its limit. I might suggest that this has become the official emotion of the US political system. It's the emotion that precedes divorce. Disgust puts its foot down and heads for the door.

While joy, happiness, and even a good surprise can make us feel lighter, these last four core emotions are heavy. Their weight is the rocks in our backpack that can create emotional fatigue, leaving us drained of the ability to experience joy and peace. This emotional fatigue is the stuff of burnout. Simply put, we get worn out from feeling heavy all the time, with no relief.

The emotionally heavy stuff of life is an equal opportunity experience. Everyone feels the weight at one time or another. When M. Scott Peck started his famous book *The Road Less Traveled* with the words "Life is difficult," no one disagreed.

In Chapter Two, I told you about my wife's cancer journey. Her breast cancer showed up for us in the middle of a very challenging season of leadership for me. Not that there's ever a convenient time for cancer to arrive, and of course it certainly wasn't all about me and my experience, but I had already been feeling an emotional depletion from the challenges of my job when the news of cancer arrived. The fear and sadness that came with the cancer diagnosis added a weight for which I wasn't prepared. Her cancer diagnosis felt like someone handed me an anvil while I was already treading water in a weighted vest.

I have heard stories from parents who have been overcome with grief and anger as they've dealt with a teenager's addiction and others who have endured the uncertainty created by their spouse's mental health challenges. I've listened to business leaders seethe with rage about trusted partners who stole from them or in some other way betrayed their trust. I've heard single parents talk about the exhausting and never-ending challenge of working to make ends meet financially while parenting their young children without any help from their estranged partner. I could go on about the internal wounds and traumas people have experienced from the hurtful behavior of family members or friends. Other times, it's the little things that add up. Criticisms and drama at work, decision fatigue on the job and at home, or the thousand-point daily to-do list that comes with raising young kids can quickly drain our reserves.

Whatever stirs these heavy core emotions, the weight that's left in their wake can wear us down and eventually take us out if we don't properly account for them.

Making a Plan

What do we do? What needs to be included in our plan to help us set down what's heavy so we can move forward with strength and joy? And in case you're wondering, yes, you do need a plan for this. We do ourselves and others around us no favors by ignoring how we feel about the rocks in our backpack or by hoping time will heal all wounds. It doesn't.

Remember Carl Fredricksen from the movie *Up*? He starts out as a curious and inquisitive, if not shy, kid who loves adventure. He marries his childhood friend and becomes a balloon vendor. But Carl picks up wounds along the way that affect him deeply. He and Ellie find out they can't have kids. In the wake of that news, they begin saving money for a "someday" adventure to Paradise Falls but have to repeatedly tap that savings to take care of everyday needs. Finally, when it seems like they are at a stage of life where they are able to go on the adventure of their dreams, Ellie becomes ill and dies. Carl is alone, dealing with his grief. When the city Carl lives in grows and development presses around the house Carl and Ellie shared, Carl becomes defensive and angry with anything that might threaten the place that houses his precious memories of Ellie. His anger and frustration eventually lead to a confrontation that earns him a court order to move out of his beloved house and into a retirement community. Carl becomes a bitter old man. Who can blame him?

We watched Carl's progression (or maybe you've watched it happen in real life with a family member or friend) with compassion and empathy. So much happened to him. No wonder he ended up a little grumpy.

As insensitive as it may sound to say, and as much as I personally identify with Carl, it's important to acknowledge that Carl didn't have to end up that way. If he had established a plan to deal with the disappointments and grief he experienced along the way, he might have been able to avoid becoming the cranky curmudgeon who needed a wild adventure with a young wilderness explorer and a talking dog named Dug in a balloon-powered house to find his joy.

How about you? Do you have a plan that is robust enough to deal with the sadness, anxiety, anger, and disgust the challenges of life stir up so you can avoid being at a three and enjoy being at an eight most of the time?

Personal Reflection and Lightning Rod People

Before we start building a plan, I want to acknowledge that I am not a mental health professional. There is much I don't know about processing emotions. I'm learning along with you. But here's what I do know: there are at least two things we all need to deal well with our heavy feelings. We can't ignore either.

First, we must set aside time to reflect. As heavy as our hurts can be, we're often unaware when they get added to our load. Just like the friends at the beach who snuck rocks into their buddy's pack, no one holds up a sign to tell us additional weight has been dropped on us. We're just doing life. We're just getting things done. We don't notice until we notice. And what we notice first typically isn't very clear. It usually shows up as our early warning signs. (Remember those?) Irritation replaces patience. Frustration replaces contentment. Anxiety replaces peace. It's all trying to tell us something's up, but we often chalk it up to a tough week or the need for a couple of days off.

You need to set aside time for personal reflection, time when you ask yourself, *What am I carrying?* Hoping what's hurting you will just fade away is a bad strategy. Just like an injury suffered at a pickup basketball game, you might want to take a closer look before shrugging it off and waiting for it to heal on its own.

I know the rationale. I've said it to myself. *I'm tough. I'll get over it. I'll just keep going and it will go away, won't it? I've got this. I can suck it up. I'll just gut it out. Rub some dirt on it. Tape an aspirin to it. There's no crying in baseball.* But while the acuteness of the pain might go away, the effect of the injury may not.

A friend of mine said, "Just because you stuff the rocks down deep in your backpack doesn't mean they're not in your backpack." A bit convicting, right? Truth is, no matter how tough you might be, if you plan on showing up at your best, you need regular, intentional practices of reflection that elevate your awareness of what you're carrying and the effect it's having on you. I'll talk more about some specific reflection practices later in this chapter.

Times of personal reflection should be partnered with time to unpack our emotional bags with those I call lightning-rod people. Lightning rods on top of buildings and houses take the heat and energy from a bolt of lightning and diffuse it into the ground so nothing gets damaged by the surge of electricity. In the same way, lightning-rod people are those who can absorb and diffuse our emotional heat and energy so we don't unload it on people at home or the office. I can't count the times I took the heat of frustration I picked up somewhere outside of my house, took it home, and unloaded it on my wife and kids in the form of uncomfortable silence or an angry outburst. Diffusing some of that energy before I got home would have made a world of difference.

Lightning-rod people hear us, see us, and empathize with us. Some may even help fix us. But their greatest contribution lies in their willingness to stand with us in our emotions and help us get some perspective without dismissing or minimizing the pain.

You can find lightning-rod people just about anywhere. I have received life-changing help from skilled, licensed therapists who helped me to reflect deeply and dig out rocks I'd carried for a long time. If you have a hunch that professional counseling might be helpful to you, I can't encourage you enough to explore it. But do this first: get recommendations from your friends, your church, or even your human resources department. Then, interview a few counselors like you would job applicants. They are going to work for you, so you want to make sure they're a good fit. Schedule thirty-minute phone calls with them and ask them how they would go about helping you with your issue. If you sense a connection, go see them a few times. If it's working and helpful, keep seeing them. If they're not helpful, it's okay to fire them and find someone else.

Beyond professionals, we can find help in the simplest of places. You might already have people like this in the circles you currently frequent. You just have to keep an eye out for them. Look for people in the following categories:

Mentors and Coaches

Ask yourself: *Who are the wise people around me?* Has there been a former boss, a professor, an athletic coach, pastor, priest, or rabbi who has taken time to listen to you and give you sage advice? These are all potential lightning-rod people. Or maybe your good friend's parent has sat with you in a difficult time and provided needed comfort and support.

When you identify a potential mentor, ask if you can take them out to lunch and ask them three important questions. They will say yes almost every time.

Friends and Partners

While not all friends will fit the category of lightning-rod people, you have some who seem to have a gift of listening and of getting you talking. They're the kind of people you look forward to having coffee with or connecting with at a ballgame or on the golf course. They're just easy to talk to. They listen and go, "Hmm, hmmm." You know they care and that they're with you, and they draw out deeper things from you.

Groups

Sometimes a group of friends or professional colleagues is more effective than any of them would be individually. Golf foursomes, hiking groups, or professional-development groups can all serve as places to talk about what you're going through. Make sure the group is okay with serving this function.

They might only offer a place to talk about specific areas of your life. For instance, a professional-development group might be the place to talk through challenges in your work life, while your hiking group or small group from church can focus more on personal issues.

When I was in the depths of my burnout, I told a counselor about my five-year journey to depletion and emotional exhaustion. When I finished the story, he asked me, "Mitch, where do you go to find empathy?" That question exposed both my deep loneliness and my need for someone to understand me. I had walled people off in an attempt to shield them from the things that were affecting me. I isolated myself because I thought the responsibilities of my job required me to carry them all alone. Bad plan. God said it was not good for us to be alone. No one was made to carry their burdens on their own.

The Practice of Processing

Below are some simple practices for personal reflection and unpacking with lightning-rod people to build into your plan of daily, weekly, monthly, periodic, and annual rhythms.

Daily

It's always a good idea to keep short accounts with your emotions.

Simple daily practices like meditation and prayer can serve the function of helping you reflect on what you might need to leave behind as you move forward. You could ask God to bring to mind what is weighing you down or stirring you up, and then you can release those things to God's care. This takes less time than you think.

If you're not spiritually inclined, use your early warning signs to take a five-minute personal inventory of things that might be weighing on you. It might sound like you asking, "What am I carrying that is making me irritated or anxious?" Then identify one step for each that turns your temperature down.

Another simple daily practice I've found helpful is to recruit some "drive time" people. These are people you can call on the way home from the office or on the way to pick up your kids from school for short fifteen-minute conversations. They function as brief check-ins on how the day went and help you verbalize frustrations or share celebrations. Practices like this help you transition from one mode (work, errands, tasks) into another (people, relationships, connections).

During certain seasons, we need something more on the daily. When a crisis is occurring or there are difficult, quickly changing circumstances, it's often good to find people who you can check in with daily. Sometimes you'll be on the receiving end of a check-in like this, and other times you'll offer it to someone else. During the weeks of Nan's chemo treatments, I would find myself asking her every day, "How are you doing today?" There was something helpful for her in that question asked that way. It wasn't just, "How are you doing?" That was too broad and vague. Adding the word "today" lets us check in around the specifics of that moment.

Questions like that can help us to reflect on and verbalize what we're carrying. Sometimes we need that every day.

Weekly

Having landing places to unpack your emotional bags on a weekly basis is helpful in keeping heavy emotions from turning toxic. The irritations we pick up during the week can grow into a root of bitterness if left unattended.

This might look like having coffee or scheduling a walking workout with a trusted friend once a week. You might use religious services every weekend as a place to do a personal check-in with yourself and others with whom you attend. It could be as simple as pausing for a few minutes before the service begins and asking some friends you attend with how their week went. When they ask you, tell them honestly. Appropriately, but honestly. You might develop needed community as others start to open up.

You can also find support by gathering with a group of friends. This does not have to be a formal support group, although if you need one, do the work to seek one out. I've found that a group of friends who meet casually each week for dinner, golf, or drinks after work can become a helpful place to "unpack some rocks."

I have a group of friends like that. They're about as "normal" as they come. Our group consists of two retired police officers, a mechanic, and a guy who negotiates contracts with labor unions (speaking of baggage picked up at work). Our ringleader has a brokerage that deals in repossessed houses. And then there's me. See? Normal.

We started getting together because the ringleader made us. He bugged the mechanic and me to have dinner with him once a week because he sensed we needed some "guy friendship" in our lives. He wasn't wrong. We still resisted for a while. Finally, we gave in when he said he'd buy dinner at a local steak joint. The three of us soon turned into six, we moved the group to one of the guy's back patios, and we've been gathering ever since.

I didn't see them as lightning-rod people first. It took a while to realize they could play that role in my life. After a particularly difficult day at work, I found myself stewing and not in a talkative mood as I drove over. When I got to the group, they asked the same insightful question they always did: "Hey, how's your week?" I was just irritated enough to tell them. And guess what? I felt lighter. I came away with more perspective. I felt heard. And I discovered the benefit of having a place to "unpack some rocks."

I now reflect on my early warning signs on the twenty-minute drive over to meet with the fellas on the patio, asking myself, *What's making me irritated or anxious this week?* When I get to the group and they ask how my week is going, I tell them. Simple as that. Some weeks, there's not much to talk about. Other times, I deeply need their support. Either way, I'm lighter for having them around.

Monthly

Reflection and unpacking practices that happen in thirty-day cycles can be more robust. You can pause longer and take a little deeper look at what has impacted you and what might be building up. The evaluation can change from what's bugging you to what's starting to characterize you. You can see more clearly if it was just a bad day or a deeper wound.

Journaling can be a particularly powerful tool to help you with this long-look reflection. Unpacking your emotions on paper can bring clarity and lightness. I use part of my time on my "day away" practice (see the chapter on rest) to journal about my early warning signs—What has made me irritated or anxious in the last month? It usually takes me a couple of pages of writing to begin to get clear about what's affected me. My practice is to write until I feel clearer and lighter. Often, if I sense I need to talk to someone about what I wrote, I'll make a note of it and ask that person to have a phone call with me or to get together over coffee.

Other monthly practices might involve connecting with your mentor or coach, attending a professional development group, scheduling a regular phone call with a trusted friend in another state, or planning for an extended time of prayer and meditation.

Periodically

You can do activities that allow for healing and restoration in your periodic rhythms of personal reflection and unpacking.

Consider scheduling a personal retreat or a day of silence every three to four months. If contemplative practices aren't really your deal, think about a weekend getaway with your spouse or a group of friends for deeper conversations in an unhurried setting. These can be easily layered on top of your periodic "no-work zone" habits we covered in the last chapter. If you take that long weekend off, use some of the time to reflect and journal while you're away.

As you engage in longer times of reflection, you will gain deeper insights about what needs to be released.

Annually

Everyone likes a fresh start. Setting aside time every year to evaluate and recalibrate lets you dump old baggage that might hinder new opportunities.

Annual habits of reflection and unpacking should address the wounds and worries of the past year that might be affecting your overall demeanor or direction. This is not a time to be in a hurry. Rather, engage tools that help you slow down and give focused attention to things that have lingered through the year or have the potential for a longer-term impact if not addressed.

I use a faith-based tool called The Great Annual Examen for this kind of long-look reflection. I set aside a substantial amount of time—sometimes a day or two—to work through the questions and write the answers in my journal. I'm careful to not rush past any of the questions. I look for patterns that are developing in the answers I give and notice "hot spots," places where my emotions might be spiking around a particular issue.

Once I complete the questions, I schedule four one-hour appointments with my counselor to go over the answers. I want us to have plenty of time to talk about anything that needs attention. I tell him about the hot spots and patterns I've seen. He asks me a lot of questions. The goal is to leave no unwanted "rocks" in my backpack.

Worth It

All of this will cost you some time and perhaps even some money. You might wonder if it's necessary.

It is.

Taking the time to look over what's in your backpack and unpack the unnecessary or depleting rocks might be just the thing that lets you climb the next hill with lightness and freedom.

NOTES

[1] Yale School of Medicine, "About Us," last updated March 25, 2025, https://medicine
.yale.edu/childstudy/services/community-and-schools-programs/center-for-emotional
-intelligence/about/.

[2] "The Science of Inside Out," *Paul Ekman Group* (blog), July 3, 2015, https://www
.paulekman.com/blog/the-science-of-inside-out/; originally published as Dacher Keltner
and Paul Ekman, "The Science of 'Inside Out,'" *The New York Times Sunday Opinion*,
July 3, 2015, https://www.nytimes.com/2015/07/05/opinion/sunday/the-science-of-inside
-out.html?partner=socialflow&smid=tw-nytimes&_r=1.

7

Receive

You don't do well when there's no air to breathe.

I found that out the hard way.

Several years ago, I was in La Paz, Bolivia, to visit two kids my wife and I sponsor through a Christian relief agency. It was humbling in ways that were easy to predict and in a couple of ways that weren't.

La Paz sits in the Andes mountains at an elevation of twelve thousand feet. The section of the city where my sponsor kids live is at thirteen thousand feet. I didn't think this was going to be a problem for me because I was in such good shape. Right. It turned out to be a little bit of a problem.

Walking on flat ground wasn't too much of an issue, but there wasn't a whole lot of flat ground to walk on. Hills and stairs were everywhere, and it wasn't long before I'd find myself breathing pretty hard. Okay, really hard. Of course I tried to hide it from my friends who were on the trip with me. I didn't want them to think I was weak. I thought I would get used to it the longer we were there. But that's not how it works. You can only go so hard when you have no air in your lungs.

Purpose works the same way.

You need purpose like you need air to breathe. Our sense of mission, meaning, and calling is fundamental to our personal well-being. Lose it, and you'll struggle to move with strength and stamina, just as I struggled at thirteen thousand feet.

In her 2013 TED talk, "How to Make Stress Your Friend," health psychologist Kelly McGonigal said, "Chasing meaning is better for your health than avoiding discomfort."[1]

As I travel and speak around the country, I come across many who are experiencing what feels like burnout but can't put their finger on why. They've got a good job, nice home, resources for travel, and things they enjoy. But they lack the sense that anything they're doing or acquiring matters that much. Nothing seems to have enough meaning in it to spark passion. They don't need more rest to gain the replenishment they need. They need more purpose.

We don't typically associate our sense of purpose and meaning with our levels of energy for work and life, but we should. Losing your "why" will leave you devoid of the kind of emotional energy that powers your motivation.

Remember in Chapter Two, we talked about how many of us worried about the premature demise of our parents in the absence of them finding something meaningful to do after they retired. I've talked with people who've admitted that they have no drive to continue in their job, marriage, and even life, because in their words, "What's the point?" You only need to hear the despair of someone who feels the deflating effect of futility in their work or life to know that we need a clear reason to exist.

Motivation, optimism, and even joy seem to run on the fuel of purpose and calling. Find your why, and you'll have a constant flow of energy available to you. Purpose and meaningful contribution put fuel in the tank.

Consider Rogelio Lopez, a municipal bus driver who drives a route every day through a notoriously tough neighborhood in Buenos Aires, Argentina. He calls it his dream job. He has become a self-appointed ambassador of joy and care for the people who ride with him. When passengers get on his bus, he greets everyone with a smile, asks them about their day, listens empathetically to their concerns, and sends them off with encouragement. When asked why he shows up each day to what could be considered a mundane job, he said, "When I sit down here [in the driver's seat], I don't exist anymore. Rogelio Lopez doesn't exist anymore, only people exist. It is my duty to treat each person who gets on my bus with dignity and kindness. For this reason, when they get on, I welcome them warmly, which is good for people. It is good for everybody."[2] "Friend Rogelio," as he calls himself, posts his routes on social media, along with pictures and videos of the places he goes and the people he meets. This allows people to intentionally get on his bus and experience his infectious energy as they start their day. Not surprisingly, he has a lot of followers. He says about his purpose:

> Worries, anxieties, all of this gets on the bus. I drive all of that when they get on. For this reason, I put myself in each person's shoes. I never think about my needs. I think about their necessities and what they go through. For this reason, I treat them with dignity. People text me telling me I am a genius. "You cheer us up. You bring us joy every morning." This is a great satisfaction to me as a professional.[3]

Friend Rogelio has found purpose, and that purpose fuels him.

The Right Kind of Stress

We've talked about the need for equal amounts of stress and replenishment and how if they get out of balance, burnout might be waiting on the horizon. And as strange as it might sound to say, that means we're going to need some stress. So, what is the right kind of stress?

Some would lead you to believe any kind of stress is bad. Don't get me wrong—an overstressed lifestyle is connected to some of the leading causes of early death. According to Mayo Clinic, heart disease, asthma, obesity, diabetes, depression, anxiety, and more are all linked to too much stress.

What's the difference between bad and good stress (which some call distress and eustress)?

Bad stress is full of fear.

Good stress is full of purpose.

Don't rush past that too quickly.

Bad stress comes from worrying that failure will result if we don't perform—and maybe even if we do. It stems from our ability to imagine the worst in any situation. The more we fear the worst, the more stressed we feel.

Good stress is different. It's fueled by our sense of purpose and meaningful contribution. Good stress knows there's work to be done but sees that work as important and full of meaning. Rogelio takes the responsibility to do his work well very seriously, but it doesn't lead to fear. He is fueled by the meaning he assigns to his work. It is his duty *and* his privilege. He is doing something important for his passengers and receives energy in return.

We need purpose and meaning to live full and vibrant lives. Purpose puts fuel in the tank. The first two rhythms we talked about—rest and release—stop the drain of energy. Our sense of purpose and meaningful contribution gives us a steady source of fuel for our most important work.

Viktor Frankl was an Austrian neurologist and psychologist who survived the death camps of World War II. In his classic book *Man's Search for Meaning*, he told of the horrific suffering he and others endured and the lessons it taught them about the meaning of life. These lessons turned into a therapeutic process known as logotherapy, which is rooted in the idea that humanity's central motivating force is having meaning in life.

Frankl shared a story that brings this idea into clear focus:

> Once, an elderly general practitioner consulted me because of his severe depression. He could not overcome the loss of his wife who had died two years before and whom he had loved above all else. Now, how can I help him? What should I tell him? Well, I refrained from telling him anything but instead confronted him with the question, "What would have happened, Doctor, if you had died first, and your wife would have had to survive you?" "Oh," he said, "for her this would have been terrible; how she would have suffered!" Whereupon I replied, "You see, Doctor, such a suffering has been spared her, and it was you who have spared her this suffering—to be sure, at the price that now you have to survive and mourn her." He said no word but shook my hand and calmly left my office. In some way, suffering ceases to be suffering at the moment it finds a meaning, such as the meaning of a sacrifice.[4]

We cannot escape this fact: we were made to matter.

Sharpening Your Purpose

What is your purpose in life?

That's one of those questions that makes us cringe a bit, isn't it? It's so broad. It's so philosophical. It feels like there's only one right answer and no right answer at the same time.

Good news: at least you get to decide what matters to you. I want to guide you with some questions that can help you get in touch with the purpose that probably already exists within you. As you work through these questions, I encourage you to slow down and reflect. This is not a time to skim the surface but to dig deep. You might find something in your answers to these questions that changes the shape of your work or the direction of your life.

What Breaks Your Heart?

I first heard this question in a sermon from Andy Stanley, the pastor of North Point Community Church in Alpharetta, Georgia, as he helped his congregation explore how they might identify their purpose and what mattered to them. It's a great question for us.

Many nonprofit organizations get started because someone saw something that broke their heart and decided right then, "Not on my watch." In Las Vegas, where I live, there are agencies that go after human traffickers and work to rescue those ensnared by bad people who treat them like property. It's the broken hearts of these brave, passionate people that give them the courage and determination to work daily against this evil.

Whether it's Martin Luther King Jr. or Rogelio the bus driver, when we let the struggles and challenges of others move us deeply, we'll find energy for days—perhaps even for our whole lives.

What breaks your heart?

What Do You Love?

What's that old saying? "Do what you love, and you'll never work a day in your life." Sounds really good. But Tim Cook, CEO of Apple, explains that's not exactly how it works. In his 2019 commencement address to Tulane University graduates, he said, "At Apple,

I learned that is a total crock. . . . You will work harder than you ever thought possible, but the tools will feel light in your hands."[5]

All work has a grind in it—even work you love—but take the love out of it, and all you're left with is grind.

In his recent book *Love + Work*, Marcus Buckingham suggests we abandon the search for work we love and instead find what we love in our work. He writes, "No, you won't ever find the perfect job, a job you love 100 percent of the time. You won't ever *do only what you love*. But you can—every single day—find some activity or situation or moment or event that you love."[6] And when we do, he explains, "In study after study, those people who reported that they had a chance to do something they loved each and every day were far more likely to be high performers and to stay in the role than those who reported that they believed in the mission of the company or liked their teammates."[7] Buckingham says all we need to be fulfilled and energized by our vocation is for 20 percent of our work to be in activities we truly love. He calls those activities "red threads." There have to be some aspects of his bus driving gig Rogelio doesn't love, but wow, is he focused on those red threads he does love.

What do you love in your work? What parts of your job, duties, and responsibilities would you do even if no one paid you? Find what you love in your work, and you'll find energy and motivation for the rest of your work.

What Gives You Energy When You Give It Energy?

Pay special attention to this, as it's one of the easiest clues to follow in finding purpose and meaning in your work and life. What have you done recently that, although it required effort, returned energy back to you? You might have come away from that activity thinking, *I'm exhausted . . . and energized!* And maybe you went home not being able to shut up about that thing you "got to do" that filled your tank instead of draining it.

I ran into a CEO at a group where I spoke who had found personal meaning in going on trips to serve people in developing nations. He did humanitarian work that alleviated human suffering and improved living conditions for under-resourced people. It was so meaningful he started recruiting people from his company to go with him. As his employees experienced a deep sense of fulfillment from serving others, they began voluntarily sacrificing their vacation time to go on these trips. They are giving energy to something that gives them energy back.

You may discover a piece of your purpose when you find your tank being filled by something that seems like it would be a drain.

What Stirs Gratitude and Celebration?

We only celebrate what matters. We're grateful for things that are deeply important to us. When you find something you want to dump a cooler of Gatorade on, you've discovered a clue to your purpose.

Have you ever taken the time to write a gratitude list? Some do this every Thanksgiving; others do a short version of it every day. Making a list of the top five or ten or twenty-five things you're the most grateful for not only focuses you on the positives, but it also reminds you of what really matters in your life, of what you want to live for.

What we celebrate tells us something important about who we are and what brings us meaning.

The Other Half of the Battle

Finding a sense of purpose is only half the battle. The other half? Keeping our sense of purpose front and center in the midst of our daily grind.

That's why this chapter is called "Receive."

We need to stand regularly under a stream of inspiration that keeps our sense of purpose and meaning in our work full and overflowing. It's easy to start a job, a business, a church, a non-profit, or even a family with a clear sense of how our purpose informs our effort. What's hard is keeping that inner flame burning white-hot when the difficulties of the endeavor conspire to snuff it out.

Without a plan to stay inspired, the problems of life and work will beat the living purpose right out of you.

You don't have to look hard to find people and institutions that have lost their way—and consequently their energy and effectiveness—because someone let the mission fade. We need a platform (a job, volunteer opportunity, hobby, etc.) through which we express our sense of purpose, and we need a pipeline, input that inspires and reinspires our personal sense of mission and calling.

Mission drift happens for a lot of reasons, but behind them is always the fact that it's easy to take passion for granted. We assume it's always going to be there. It's important, and we feel it deeply and talk about it convincingly, so how could we ever lose sight of it?

Seems unlikely. But we do.

And when we do, what was once so crucial and integral to who we are and what we're all about can quickly get snowed under in a blizzard of less important things.

When I was a teenager, my brother and I went hiking with our twenty-year-old next-door neighbor, Leonard, up above Wawona Tunnel in Yosemite National Park. He secured a permit and filed plans for us to hike up past Old Inspiration Point, the famous location where Ansel Adams took an iconic picture, with Half Dome on the right and El Capitan looming on the left. We were going to hike and camp for three days as we made our way along the trail that leads toward Half Dome.

The hiking part was great, but we weren't prepared for the cold nights.

No one told me there was going to be snow or that we would be sleeping in it. Once the sun went down, the fire was our only friend. It was a demanding friend, wanting to be fed constantly. Frankly, we were too cold to do it. No one wanted to move away from the dying fire to get wood to keep it going for even a little while, much less gather enough to keep it going all night. It didn't matter how big our fire was to begin with; if we wanted to keep it going through the cold night, we needed a plan.

Long before the cold set in and our fatigue drove us to laziness, we should have figured out a way to supply the fire with what it needed to keep from going out.

You see where I'm going with this?

No matter how noble, altruistic, or important your work, eventually, the fire of meaning that drew you to it and motivated your efforts will need to be restoked. Do you have a plan to provide a regular supply of inspiration that will keep the fire of your purpose burning hot even through difficult circumstances?

Be prepared: identifying intentional habits that inspire our purpose isn't easy. More often, inspiration finds us, or we stumble across it accidentally.

We get inspired when something around us resonates with something inside of us and propels us to what's ahead of us. The more we can tune our awareness to the voices that speak to our soul, the better our plan to receive the inspiration we need will be.

Daily

One of the best ways to stay focused on living your purpose is to use morning rituals to set the direction of your day.

If you're a spiritual person, morning devotional readings and time for prayer can help you reconnect with what is most meaningful before the distractions of the day start to pull at you. Receiving truth and direction from God each morning raises your focus to the highest priorities, above the daily trivia that can sweep it away.

You can use meditation practices to help quiet your mind and set your intention for the day. Take even just ten to fifteen minutes a day to quietly reflect on your life priorities and how you intend to use the hours in your day.

When you adopt daily practices like these, you will repeatedly remind yourself who you are and why you're here so you can take purpose-fueled energy with you into the challenges of that day.

Weekly

Just as the body needs the right kind of regular sustenance to fuel it, so does your purpose, so think of weekly receiving practices as the diet that nourishes your calling.

Ask yourself: Who are the voices that speak life-giving words of truth to you? It might be your pastor, priest, or rabbi, or maybe an author or leader with whom you particularly resonate. Listening to audiobooks or podcasts in the car during your commute or during one of your workouts on the treadmill can add those voices to your weekly diet.

Do you read books or listen to audiobooks? Why not choose books that resonate with your purpose? Read or listen to biographies of great leaders, and let them stir your leadership gift. Read or listen to helpful books that challenge you toward personal growth in areas you want to improve. I constantly use books to inspire me to fresh passion for personal growth and the work I do to help others.

These weekly inputs will keep you fueled and focused for your most important contributions.

Monthly

When it comes to keeping our "why" burning hot, we need opportunities to express our purpose on a regular basis in other ways than just our work. These expressions become part of the platform on which we live out our calling, places where we expend energy to gain energy.

Volunteering in an area that connects with our calling is an easy way to stoke the fires of our personal purpose. But be careful. I spoke to one executive who started volunteering at a shelter that serves meals to the homeless. She loved working in the kitchen, prepping the food, and serving it to those in the shelter, but when the staff of the shelter discovered what she did for a living, they wanted her to help with the administrative side of the work. Because serving the homeless was a passion of hers, she said yes, and she found herself quickly wearing out rather than being energized by it. She wisely moved back to the kitchen. To be clear, volunteering isn't all about us. That defeats the purpose too. But everyone wins when we find a place to serve at the intersection of what others need and what we care deeply about.

Other monthly habits might include connecting with mentors or hosting a lunch with leaders in your field or people in your neighborhood. Professional development or peer coaching groups might be another option for executives and marketplace leaders. I have had the great privilege of both being a member of and a speaker for Vistage Worldwide, the largest peer coaching organization in the world for business leaders of midsize companies. I've found the monthly meetings create a helpful rhythm of input and practice that allows me to revisit my calling regularly. Groups like this (whether formal or informal) can put us in conversation with peers who help us stay focused and fueled in the area of our passion.

Periodically

You'll discover three- or four-month cycles to be useful to insert experiences that remind you of and rekindle your sense of calling and purpose that can so easily get beaten down in the day-to-day challenges of work and life.

Some plan a walk in the woods or a kayak trip down a local river to reflect on their place in the world and their desire to make a meaningful contribution to it.

Others schedule time to comb through the neighborhood bookstore to gather inspirational reading material they'll dive into in the next quarter.

I use this periodic time frame to connect with specific kinds of mentors who speak to longer perspectives in my life. Some mentors are helpful in day-to-day or week-to-week problem solving and guidance, while others are more valuable in longer-look, more philosophical issues about where your career and life are headed. These types of conversations require preparation. The conversations will be richer if you take the time to prewrite questions and think through the issues you'll talk about.

Annually

There is great benefit in annual markers and checkpoints to measure progress and stagnation. Look at your purpose in a once-a-year time frame to help you assess what might have legitimately shifted in the past year and what might have unintentionally drifted.

Personal retreats or intentional days of annual reflection can help you realign and reignite your calling. I have used both professional conferences and personal spiritual retreats as venues to receive input that sharpens my sense of mission.

Perhaps you've done some life planning with a certified coach or with a helpful mentor or friend. Have you revisited that lately? Try using the week between Christmas and New Year's Day every year to take a fresh look at your life plan and make some adjustments or recommitments.

Everyone loves a fresh start, and annual rhythms give you a chance to re-up for the personal mission that will pour fuel into your tank.

It's Not About You

One last thought about the calling that fuels us: it'll never be about you.

Purpose, it turns out, is always the most filling and most fulfilling when it's about elevating others. We will only wear out trying to elevate ourselves. We will always gain energy from the work we do to lift others. There is no shortage of research to validate this. In his article titled "Here's the Science: Helping Others Is the Key to Happiness," Joshua Becker points to a study done at the UMass Chan Medical School by research professor Carolyn Schwartz. She was trying to identify ways in which people with multiple sclerosis could be better helped by things like peer-support phone calls. What she found was that those who offered support to others were helped more than the people who received the support. She said, "A newly emerging school of thought suggests that a simple, age-old principle may be part of both the prevention and the cure: Help others to help yourself."[8]

In the same article, Becker quotes Stephen Post, a research professor of bioethics at Case Western Reserve University, who said, "One of the best ways to overcome stress is to do something to help someone else."[9]

Every feel-good video you've ever seen is about someone helping someone else in need, using their resources for the benefit of another.

Jesus told us in the New Testament that the world works far better when we give rather than just receive (see Acts 20:35).

I realize this may be a weird thing to point out in a chapter called "Receive," but when our receiving is done for the purpose of staying inspired to live our purpose for the good of others, we'll find ourselves giving and receiving more than we could have imagined.

It's a great truth that when we give, we receive more. It's a greater truth that when we give, we receive more so we can give even more. It's a beautiful cycle.

Once more from Viktor Frankl: "The more one forgets himself—by giving himself to a cause to serve or another person to love—the more human he is and the more he actualizes himself."[10]

NOTES

[1] Kelly McGonigal, "How to Make Stress Your Friend," TED, June 2013, https://www.ted.com/talks/kelly_mcgonigal_how_to_make_stress_your_friend?subtitle=en.

[2] "Watch Argentina's Happiest Bus Driver Make His Passengers' Day," *USA Today*, May 22, 2024, https://www.usatoday.com/videos/life/humankind/2024/05/22/argentinas-happiest-bus-driver-shares-positive-vibes-with-passengers/73719422007/. For the full video, see Newzee, "Meet the Happiest Bus Driver of Argentina," YouTube, April 19, 2024, https://youtu.be/11PebFHVN88.

[3] Newzee, "Meet the Happiest Bus Driver of Argentina."

[4] Viktor Frankl, *Man's Search for Meaning* (Verlag für Jugend und Volk, 1946; Beacon Press, 2006), 51. Citations refer to the Beacon Press edition.

[5] Catherine Clifford, "Apple CEO Tim Cook: 'If You Love What You Do, You Will Never Work a Day in Your Life' Is 'Total Crock,'" CNBC Make It, May 18, 2019, https://www.cnbc.com/2019/05/18/apple-ceo-tim-cook-if-you-love-what-you-do-you-will-never-work-a-day-in-your-life-is-total-crock.html.

[6] Marcus Buckingham, *Love + Work: How to Find What You Love, Love What You Do, and Do It for the Rest of Your Life* (Harvard Business Review Press, 2022), 190.

[7] Buckingham, *Love + Work*, 187.

[8] Joshua Becker, "Here's the Science: Helping Others Is the Key to Happiness," Becoming Minimalist, May 27, 2022, https://www.becomingminimalist.com/helping-science.

⁹Becker, "Here's the Science."
¹⁰Frankl, *Man's Search for Meaning*, 110.

8

Recreate

"Why do we need to have fun?"

I had been speaking on the topic of burnout for a while, sharing insights I'd gained from my own crash, and would always ask this question. It seemed relevant as I prompted my audience to think about why they might want to include some enjoyable activities in their replenishment routines.

But there was an issue: I didn't know the answer.

I had the same vague idea most of us have. Fun is good because fun makes us happy. I mean, who doesn't want to have fun? As kids, we pursued play like it was our full-time job. We took our playtime pretty seriously, inventing games and rounding up friends to join us. As we got older, we realized we could afford a bigger version of the fun we had as kids. Bikes turned into motorcycles, playing Little League Baseball turned into season tickets to Major League Baseball games, dressing up our dolls turned into shopping trips to fashion outlets. Cyndi Lauper only had it half right—it's not just girls; it seems like we all just want to have fun.

Sure, let's have some fun. How hard is that?

This may seem a little odd. Insisting we need to be intentional about adding enjoyable activities to our schedules might sound like telling grizzly bears they need to be careful to add some salmon to their diet.

For the most part, we get that having fun is an important part of an emotionally healthy life. When you think of someone you know who never has any fun, you're pretty sure there must be something wrong with them. You'd be right. Enjoyment and recreation seem like at least a piece of what we need to have a fulfilling life.

Even though the answer to *Why do we need to have fun?* escaped me, the need for it did not. In one group of business leaders I spoke to, an executive confessed through tears that he hadn't taken a vacation in ten years. Everyone in the room groaned in sadness for the missed family moments and the prolonged fatigue they immediately assumed this leader had endured. They all knew there was something deeply wrong with working for that long with no break to enjoy life.

Again, if it's so obvious, why do we need to talk about this?

Even though we know better, we don't necessarily do better. We trade in playtime for productivity because everyone knows you can't have both. Right? How many of us were told as kids to stop goofing around and get to work? So we did. Because that's what grown-ups do. According to Statista, a global data-gathering firm, the average hours per day spent on leisure and sports dips by over an hour once you leave adolescence behind and enter the twenty-five- to fifty-four-year-old range.[1] Somewhere along the way, we kids quit playing and traded away our recreation.

When work time competes withs fun time, work time almost always wins. I get why. Work time keeps food on the table and a roof over our heads. It pays for the necessities that responsible, adult life requires—things like health insurance, car insurance, homeowners insurance, life insurance. (Being an adult is a lot about insurance!) Work time eventually lets us buy more of the stuff we're sure we're supposed to have, and that makes it the priority.

Also, if you subscribe to a "survival of the fittest" view of life, you'll conclude that fun isn't a helpful way to spend your time. Drop your guard for a bit to indulge some amusement, and you'll find yourself on the dinner menu of a predator. Fun will distract you from the important stuff. Fun can get you blindsided. Not only is fun not necessary; it's straight-up dangerous. It seems wiser to just knuckle down and get to work. Better to not take the chance of frivolity turning into failure.

And this might be why you're burning out.

While you may have never consciously adopted a "survival of the fittest" point of view, you might be driven by it. You might (secretly) think your ability to keep your head down and soldier on while others need to take vacations and days off makes you more noble. You may even consider it your best quality.

It's not.

Don't get me wrong—there is great nobility in hard work. But there is no nobility in overwork and a joyless life.

What's the Answer?

Why do we need to have fun?

I asked that question to a speaker and corporate coach I ran into at a business leaders meeting I regularly attend. He was different from the other speakers we typically had. He didn't talk about sales strategies or hiring practices. No mention of artificial intelligence applications or personality profiles. He talked about people and life and the nature of truth. He explained how we can easily slip into the "victim" role and how that mindset debilitates us. His name was Todd Musselman, and he seemed like the kind of guy who would know the answer to a question like *Why do we need to have fun?*

He did.

"Fun drags us into the present."

Whoa. Didn't see that coming.

He explained, "You never have fun except when you are fully present."

I immediately began to recall moments of laugh-out-loud fun and deep enjoyment, and I realized he was right. I was only there, in that moment, and nowhere else.

He continued, "You've never had fun when you were preoccupied or distracted. In fact, you've never had anything significant happen to you when you weren't fully present. You've never had a significant conversation when you were checking your email or staring at your phone."

Thanks, Todd.

Here's what I took away from that question-and-answer session with Todd: recreation, fun, play, entertainment, and enjoyment take us away from the work that drains us and create space for us to recover.

It's no mystery that the hardest work to stop doing is the work going on in our minds. It's what keeps you up at night and distracts you during the day. It pulls you away from important moments with your spouse, kids, friends, and family. Shutting down the mental workspace when there's work left to be done is next to impossible without something else to give your attention to. And that something else must be mentally invigorating and emotionally captivating enough to occupy your attention. The old-fashioned word people used to use for recreation was *diversion.* In the 1964 Disney classic, *Mary Poppins,* the magical British nanny promised her new employer, Mr. Banks, that the games she would engage the children in would be "extremely diverting."[2] The activities would be captivating enough to redirect their attention away from mundane work and onto something more mentally and emotionally stimulating.

For our minds and bodies to find renewal, we need something diverting enough to drag us into the present.

In those moments, fun comes to the rescue.

When we're really having fun, we're only there, fully present in that moment. Fun, it turns out, is the quickest, easiest way for you to leave work behind for a while, disengage yourself from the mental (and physical) tasks that deplete your energy, and find some refreshment. In the same way we said purpose energizes us, fun also puts fuel in the tank because it engages joy. That's why they call it enjoyment.

As good as it is to have some fun now and again, and as easy as that seems to do, we still have to intentionally choose to let ourselves be present and enjoy it. While engaging in recreation is the quickest way to shut off our preoccupation with work and to rest our weary minds and souls, it is not automatic.

Even the most enjoyable activities are no match for a will that's determined to keep working. While fun might drag us into the present, our adaptive challenges (as we have defined them) will do everything they can to drag us away from it.

- ► Toxic responsibility can keep us chained to our desk so we can't disengage enough to enjoy a ballgame.
- ► Compulsive achievement will urge us to jump on that phone call from the important client in the middle of our kid's school play.

It's in the moments where we try to build rhythms of recreation that our adaptive challenges might scream the loudest. They want to keep us doing the "safe" thing—working. Our hyper-urgent soul will try to make it abundantly clear that fun is frivolous and maybe even a total waste of time.

If we're going to get the full benefit of recreation, we not only have to select activities fun enough to be diverting, but we must also do the work to turn down the voices of our adaptive challenges so we can fully engage with fun.

What's Fun to You?

What do you like to do for fun? What type of recreation provides an escape hatch for you to leave work behind and savor some enjoyment?

Back in Chapter Five, you made a list of things you find restful. Take a look at your list, and notice which are actually recreational in nature. Those activities are a good starting point to identify what can help recreate us. You might want to do some reflecting and experimenting to see what else you can add to the list.

The older we get, the more our once-enjoyable activities get filtered off our list. Or we decide—maybe too quickly—that certain types of activities aren't for us. I'm amazed at how many people, both young and old, have discovered pickleball. Who knew pickleball was so much fun? You might want to give it, or any number of other activities, a try.

Not only do we need to identify the types of activities that renew us; we also need to find the correct frequency. Things that help us if we do them once a month can become burdensome if we try to make them happen once a week. Activities that are great to do annually might lose their romance if we did them monthly.

For example, did you know that it's possible to "over-golf" yourself? It is. If you are a golfer, you might have a hard time believing that. But I found out the hard way that too much golf—at least for me—was more depleting and defeating than it was helpful.

During one stretch, a couple of friends and I all had Mondays off work, so we started playing three of the four Mondays every month. Now, I'm no Tiger Woods, but I was playing to a pretty respectable (for me) ten handicap. The more we played, the more consistent my game became and the more fun I was having, not to mention I was beating both of my friends most of the time. See? Fun!

Then came the fateful day.

I had this brilliant idea that if I was getting so good at golf and enjoying it this much playing three times a month, surely adding a round on the fourth week would make me better and the game more fun. I also decided if I put up a practice net in my garage and hit a few balls every day, I'd be even better and would enjoy it even more. It was a great plan. What could possibly go wrong?

What went wrong was that when my score didn't get better like I thought it should after all that practice, it kind of made me mad. Okay, it royally ticked me off. In about two months, golf went from being a source of enjoyment to an exercise in frustration. I got so irritated that I almost sold my clubs. I quit playing for about eight months. At one point, I thought I'd never play again.

What happened? How did this recreational activity that had been a source of enjoyment turn into such a drag?

Overuse.

Too much of a good thing wasn't a good thing. The type of activity wasn't the problem. Golf is a great game for me. The amount of focus and concentration required to play the game takes my mind away from work. Add to that being outdoors on green grass (that I don't have to mow, by the way), and under the warmth of the sun, and I am thoroughly diverted. But I almost lost all that because I got the frequency wrong. When golf went from being a weekly pastime to being a daily regimen, it stopped helping and started hurting. It went from being a joy to being a job.

You might think recreational activities would be hard to mess up. They're not. The right plan of recreation will be as individual as you are and might take a little trial and error. When a busy leader or parent tries to add some fun to the mix and has a bad experience, they often give up on it wholesale. The less than helpful experience confirms their misguided belief that fun is frivolous and work more important. They come to the mistaken conclusion that recreation is a big waste of time, but nothing could be further from the truth.

As strange as it sounds, you have to keep working at having fun. Fun isn't automatic, but it is essential.

Rhythms and Scale

Just like it matters to get the frequency of our fun dialed in, it's also important to sync up the right scale and rhythm of our activities. Because of this, you need to use the framework of daily, weekly, monthly, periodic, and annual rhythms to help clarify the type and scale of the activities you'll add to your plan.

Here's what I mean: one of the most common answers I get to the question "What's your favorite form of recreation?" is hiking. Seems like a global pandemic helped getting into the great outdoors on a footpath make a huge comeback.

You like hiking. Great. The real question is, What kind of hiking do you mean? Is it a day hike in the mountains that requires a plan for lunch and a significant water supply? Or is it hiking through the neighborhood park with the dog in tow? Or do you mean pulling a permit, heading to a national park, and solo hiking for three days? Depending on your answer, it might be a daily or weekly activity or one that you'd plan for annually. See the difference? Perhaps you need both the simple one-hour daily hike and an annual, multiday trek through the wilderness. Different levels of the same activity offer different benefits.

Recognizing the difference grows our competence in managing stress and replenishment.

I mentioned how I got my rhythm of golf out of whack. I took something that was a good weekly activity and tried to make it a daily routine. These days, golf is helpful to me about once a month. How often do I need to play golf to be at an eight 80 percent of the time? I found out the hard way that it's good to know.

Let me remind you that we keep our tank full by balancing the amount and type of stress we experience with the right type and amount of replenishment. Just as you can get too much stress and not enough replenishment, experiencing too much replenishment—like the wrong amount or type of recreation—can also be a problem. You need to pay attention to the kind of benefits you're receiving from the types and amounts of recreational activities you've chosen.

I've discovered that during the fall, one activity that gives me great joy is following college football. I have my team, but I also enjoy following the other teams chasing down the national championship each year. And while I do other recreational activities that are more physical in nature, the college football season allows me some passive fun. It is very effective in dragging me away from work and into the present.

I used to feel guilty about spending (wasting) time wrapped up in a game I've had to learn to admit has no real consequence to the world. But once I understood its function in giving me a weekly rhythm of drawing back, recovering energy, and experiencing enjoyment, I leaned in guilt free.

But because I like watching college football so much, the healthy weekly escape can easily turn into a distraction. The weekly enjoyment of the games can become daily (hourly?) dives into coaches' polls, game analysis, and player profiles, to my own detriment. And while it would be really fun to travel to watch my team play in person, I'd have to take a careful look at how often I should make such a big investment of time so the positive effect of the recreation wouldn't become a negative experience of mismanaged replenishment. Watching the games every week from home is awesome. A periodic trip to a game might be fine. A monthly outing would be too much for me right now.

Too much replenishment—especially in the form of recreation—can rob us of the kind of purpose-filled stress that makes life and work meaningful. Many convince themselves that because their work is so stressful, they deserve whatever fun they can muster to balance the scales. That would be a mistake. Overdosing on recreation can be just as damaging as not having any fun at all. It's important to know what type and level of activity gives us the right dose of enjoyment to keep showing up at our best.

Daily

Daily activities should differ from weekly and monthly routines in scale and function. Daily fun is meant to help us start or finish the day with enjoyment and a healthy purging of stress. It can create enthusiasm and anticipation for the coming day or close your day out well. Adding an after-dinner walk around the block or working on a craft project (my mom crocheted and knitted to her heart's content at the end of every day) can help move you in the direction of your true north.

I usually caution people about assuming their exercise routines are a part of their recreational life. They can be if the exercise is fun and enjoyable. A morning run or Pilates class can be a great way to clear your mind or help you get your motor running. But if exercise is not something that brings enjoyment, if it feels more rigorous than it does refreshing, you might not want to count it as part of your recreation.

Weekly

Weekly recreation can create the right kind of "laps" in your work/rest rhythms. In the same way you'd draw a hammer back to create potential energy before swinging it at a nail, weekly patterns of recreation give you a moment to back away from work and reload your energy before unleashing it on the tasks of your week. Weekly escapes to the golf course, bike path, farmers market, backyard garden, or garage woodshop help to drag us away from the mental work, which is otherwise hard to shut off, and into the present—just as our friend Todd Musselman told us it would. We seem to be created with a need for a weekly pause to engage in a diverting activity that allows us to blow out the mental cobwebs and prep for another go-round. Many major religions include the practice of a weekly day off to rest and worship. Of the Ten Commandments, it's the commandment regarding the Sabbath that got the most ink (see Exod. 20:3–17.) There's something instructive about that.

Monthly

Monthly diversions give you more time to reset and provide the kind of break needed for recovery and maintenance. Think of it as a bye week in a football season—a longer period of time off—to get away from the stresses and strains of the daily/weekly grind and to let routine injuries heal.

Consider taking your date night to a new level and find that fancier restaurant or go on a picnic. Your love for the outdoors can take you on a longer hike—maybe one that requires a permit and group of friends. Maybe your love for cooking turns into a gathering where you invite friends to prep the meal with you.

Monthly recreation should be big enough to look forward to.

Periodic and Annual

Periodic and annual vacations give you substantial time to remember that life is more than just work. It's during these longer-term breaks that we plan memory-making fun that lets us live in our true north for an extended, largely unhindered length of time. It's these moments that ingrain in us the muscle memory of what our true north feels like so we can use it as a reference point for the rest of the year.

Consider leaving your laptop at home. Do something that will create cherished memories and leave a mark on you and whoever is with you. Figure out what kind of vacations are truly refreshing, as opposed to the type that just make you feel like you need a vacation from your vacation.

Joy Matters

I'm naturally a pretty serious guy. At least that's what I told myself.

The truth is, somewhere along the way, I had convinced myself it was better to be serious all the time because it didn't feel good to not be taken seriously.

Growing up, I'd been the comedian of the family. I was the kid at the dinner table who could get everyone laughing. I liked to memorize the jokes from the comedy section of *Reader's Digest* and then entertain the family to fill moments of awkward silence. I enjoyed being fun and funny.

One day, I received a backhanded compliment about my humor. I'm not sure what was actually said, but what I heard was, "Other people are smart and competent; you're funny." That was the last day for a long time I believed being fun and funny were good things. Serious and competent took the top spots on my "best things to be" list.

Years into my adult life, I realized I'd become just what I set out to be: serious and competent. And not fun. Slowly, over time, every fun activity had faded from my calendar in favor of work. Important work, sure. Work that provided food and shelter, no less. But I had become the dull boy the "all work and no play" lifestyle produces. No one was accusing me of being joyful, and they were right. Joy just wasn't that important to this serious person.

To make matters worse, the Christian faith teaches that one of the top qualities that naturally emerges in you as you learn to walk in step with Jesus is—you guessed it—joy. In fact, in the New Testament letter he wrote to the Galatians, the apostle Paul pointed to a list of things that would be produced in a person's life who stayed in step with the Holy Spirit. Joy was number two on that list. Yet I had next to none.

And then I crashed.

There's something about running into your own wall that makes you reevaluate your trajectory. In my pit of burnout, I had time to rethink some of the things I'd told myself about how life worked best. I realized I had set up a false dichotomy. I thought I had to choose either competent and serious or fun and funny. I didn't.

Why do we need to have fun? Because we were made for joy. In the New Testament letter from the apostle Paul to his young apprentice, Timothy, Paul is instructing Timothy on the things he should teach people about what matters most in life. In 1 Timothy 6:17, he writes: "Command those who are rich in this present world not to be arrogant nor to put their hope in wealth, which is so uncertain . . ."

Good advice for anyone. He continues:

". . . but to put their hope in God, who richly provides us with everything for our . . ."

I'm ready for him to say "usefulness" or "daily needs." You know, something serious and important. But what he actually says is this:

". . . who richly provides us with everything for our enjoyment."

I don't think this is an encouragement to be frivolous, but I do believe it's telling us our lives were meant to include enjoyment—joy, fun, and laughter.

What's fun to you? When are you planning on getting some of that?

NOTES

[1]"Average Hours Per Day Spent on Leisure and Sports by U.S. Population by Age from 2010 to 2023," Statista, July 22, 2024, https://www.statista.com/statistics/189597/daily-average-time-spent-on-sports-and-leisure-by-age-in-the-us/.

[2]*Mary Poppins*, directed by Robert Stevenson (Buena Vista, 1964).

9

Relate

"No camera crews."

"No gimmicks."

"The ultimate test of human will."[1]

That's the description for a television show that is hard for me to watch and to not watch at the same time. The premise, on certain days, sounds pretty good to me, but I still can't believe people want to be on this show.

Survive for as long as you can in the wild.

That's it.

The contestants get to take standard outdoor clothing, a first aid kit, emergency supplies, up to ten pieces of survival gear from a predetermined list, and a satellite phone that can only be used for a medical emergency or if a contestant wants to bail. All you have to do? Make it in the wilderness longer than the nine other people who signed up for the challenge. Do that, and you win half a million dollars. They tell the contestants up front that the filming of the show could last for up to a year.

Oh, and the catch? You have to survive alone.

That's what the show is called. *Alone.*

There are no show producers or camera people following you around. No visits from locals or other contestants. The only human contact occurs when a medic comes every seven to fourteen days for a twenty-minute health check to determine if you're fit to continue.

Your only job is to stay alive.

The answer to the question you want to ask is one hundred days. That's the longest anyone has survived alone before tapping out. It may not surprise you to learn that feat was accomplished in a special season of the show when they offered one million dollars to anyone who could last one hundred days. Without that added incentive, the longest time alone was eighty-seven days.

True wilderness survival is tough no matter how many people are with you, but there is something uniquely unsettling about the prospect of being truly isolated for that long, alone with only your thoughts and the animals who'd like to eat you.

The point of the reality show is that people can't make it long on their own, but the real reality is that we try to do it all the time.

Take it to the Limit

There's something satisfying about being self-sufficient.

We like to push the boundaries of independence. There is a very real part of us that can (and arguably should be able to) handle a lot on our own. Plus, we feel less vulnerable when we're not dependent on others for our well-being. Rugged individualism is practically a national ethic. We wear it as a badge of honor, and we think a little less of those who seem to need others too much.

But as with our other adaptive challenges, we can take what can be helpful in the right amounts and overuse it to our detriment. Individualism can quickly lead to isolation. The lone wolf can easily end up lonely. In a 2023 article from the US Department of Health and Human Services, US Surgeon General Dr. Vivek Murthy cautioned, "Our epidemic of loneliness and isolation has been an underappreciated public health crisis that has harmed individual and societal health. Our relationships are a source of healing and well-being hiding in plain sight—one that can help us live healthier, more fulfilled, and more productive lives." The article points out that, "Even before the onset of the COVID-19 pandemic, approximately half of US adults reported experiencing measurable levels of loneliness."[2]

All that alone time has pretty devastating results, even if we aren't trying to solo survive in the wilderness. The article goes on to say, "The physical health consequences of poor or insufficient connection include a 29 percent increased risk of heart disease, a 32 percent increased risk of stroke, and a 50 percent increased risk of developing dementia for older adults. Additionally, lacking social connection increases risk of premature death by more than 60 percent."[3]

There's good news: we can avoid much of that by simply prioritizing connection with others. In his studies of aging and longevity, explorer and author Dan Buettner and his team identified five "Blue Zones" around the world where people live extraordinarily long and healthy lives. Buettner identified nine lifestyle characteristics people in places like Okinawa, Japan; Ikaria, Greece; and Loma Linda, California seem to have in common. In his book *The Blue Zones Secrets for Living Longer: Lessons from the Healthiest Places on Earth*, Buettner reported that of these "Power 9" characteristics of Blue Zone communities, three have everything to do with the quality and quantity of social relationships. Blue Zone people prioritize time with their loved ones—giving special attention to their spouses and children. They curate social circles that promote healthy lifestyle choices like diet and exercise, and they tend to belong to faith-based communities—church attendance extends their lives four to fourteen years beyond the lifespans of people who do not regularly go to church.[4]

Bottom line: if you want to live a longer and healthier life, alone is not the way to go. Maybe we should believe what God said in the beginning: "It is not good for . . . man to be alone" (Gen. 2:18). We were made for relationships.

The Drift Apart

Most of us don't set out in the direction of isolation. "Live a lonely life" is not on anyone's bucket list.

I never intended to separate myself from other people. Admittedly, I'm an introvert by nature, which means I tend to gain and recover energy in times of quiet solitude. But that doesn't mean I don't like being around people. It just means that after spending time with others, I then need some time on my own to recoup the energy I expended.

Before my burnout set in, I had what seemed like a great community around me. I had close friends I played golf with and a large group of people from my work at a large church who I chatted with regularly. And, of course, my wife and kids were always there waiting for me at the end of the day. From the outside, you'd probably conclude I had all the relational connection I needed.

But along the way, I became increasingly solitary. As responsibilities at work shifted and I stepped into a more executive role that required an elevated level of confidentiality and discretion, I found myself with fewer and fewer people I could talk to—or so I thought. Because much of my job focused on personnel management, I dealt regularly with conflicts and issues that couldn't be discussed outside of a very small circle. To make matters worse, the more I dealt with "people problems" in the job, the more I began to believe that people were problems. There were those who made mistakes I had to clean up, so I backed away. Others became hard to trust, so I built a wall. I smiled politely and told people I cared (and I did), but I always walked away by myself to deal on my own with whatever they dropped on my plate. My toxic responsibility insisted that was my job. My ego said I should be able to handle it on my own. My introverted temperament told me more time by myself was the answer.

And the drift was on.

Solitude became my sanctuary and isolation my own private island of escape. I was a contestant in my own personal survival game of "Alone."

Not only did I neglect the support I needed to unpack my emotional baggage (as we talked about in Chapter Six), but I also allowed time for the simple enjoyment of friends and family to evaporate. I was a long way down the path I'd seen others take, and it didn't end up anywhere good.

Friends

A report by the National Academies of Sciences, Engineering, and Medicine highlighted that more than a third of adults over forty-five years old and nearly a fourth of adults over sixty-five are considered to be socially isolated.[5]

Anecdotally, I've watched aging executives increasingly disconnect from friends the more successful they become. The "lonely at the top" cliché becomes a reality as they gain organizational authority and positional elevation that separates them from their peers. Genuine friendship becomes harder to find, and many of these executives choose not to find time for them.

It's not just executives. Many of us follow that same drift into isolation. Stay-at-home parents can find themselves spending all their time with people under four feet tall because of the logistical difficulties of getting together with adult friends. Military personnel who move to new duty stations every three or four years can grow fatigued at the prospect of having to build new relational circles again and again. The work-from-home phenomenon we all discovered during the COVID-19 pandemic provided the convenience of not working in an office and the isolation that came with it.

The problem is that a lack of relational connection with friends and family who refresh our souls and fill our tanks will contribute to our burnout.

Why?

We were made for relationship.

But not just any kind of relationship.

We have plenty of relationships with people who provide for our functional needs—doctors, accountants, car wash operators, food servers, and delivery drivers. We might be friendly with many of these people, but those functional relationships are very different from the intimate, vulnerable, self-sacrificing, soul-filling relationships we get from true friends. Jesus taught, "There is no greater love than to lay down one's life for one's friends" (John 15:13 NLT). Turn that statement around, and you understand the depth of genuine friendship: true friends are those who lay their life down for you. That's probably way different than your relationship with the barista who makes your Frappuccino or the person who sells you car insurance.

We need regular doses of relational connectivity with the people in our lives who fit Jesus's definition of friendship—those who pour themselves out for us and for whom we do the same. They are the people we connect with on a soul level and with whom we experience deep enjoyment and meaningful connection.

Who are the people who make your life richer and refresh your soul?

You need these kinds of friends for this important reason: they help you feel like your true self. They remind you of who you really are. You not only like who they are, but you like who you are when you're with them. They bring out the best in you by giving the best of who they are to you. And you do the same for them. These types of relationship are always mutual, never one-sided. They're not about a transaction—only about what they do for you, or what you give to them, or whose turn it is. They're always about the connection. We often say about them that somewhere along the way they became family.

Do you have people like this? You may want to start making a list, and you might want to start making some phone calls and sending some texts to thank those people for being those people. If, as you've been reading, some people's faces flashed through your mind, you may want to offer a prayer of gratitude for them. They are a gift.

In my experience, there are a ton of ingredients that go into the mix of making life-giving friendships, and one stands out above the others: vulnerability. So many other pieces of deep friendship hang on this one quality. Vulnerability, as I see it, is a willingness to be unguarded to the point that I can be affected by you. If that's true, you and I will never have friendships deeper than our willingness to risk being disappointed, rejected, or changed by each other. I haven't really let you in until you can hurt me or help me, until you can move me or melt me. That's vulnerability. When we can be vulnerable with another, we experience ultimate safety, but getting there is a little scary. That's why many people stop short of the kind of soul-filling friendship that puts wind in their sails.

If you don't have many relationships that fit this description, you can start building them now. As former Georgia State Game & Fish Commission director George Bagby said, "It has been said that the best time to plant a tree is thirty years ago, the second-best time is today."[6] Deep friendships are important; the joy is in the journey together, and the richness is in the shared memories made along the way.

Other Friends

Here's the rest of the story.

Even though we need the blessing of soul-deep friendships, they aren't the only kind of relationship we need to help keep our tank full. There are many other levels of relationship that also create enjoyment and fulfillment. For instance, we need a healthy dose of what I call "fun friends." Yep, these are people with whom we have a lot of fun. They're the ones we might call to jump in with us on all the activities we talked about in the last chapter on recreation. We go on hikes, go fishing, go to ball games, or go skiing with these kinds of friends. They're a ton of fun to be around, and they probably feel the same way about you. We might not share the kind of vulnerability with them that would take our relationship deeper, but we would be missing something without time together.

There's also a place for "support friends"—people you get together with for mutual support and encouragement. These might include parents who gather to encourage each other as they raise young kids or friends who gather for Bible study.

In every type of friendship, we need to appreciate the simple goodness of being together and the value other people bring to our lives. There is so much good to be found in the people around us.

Rhythms

The one regret I hear most from people (and myself) about all this is that they just don't spend enough time with their friends.

If friendship grows from the seeds of vulnerability, then time is the soil it grows in. Relational depth never develops quickly.

Experiencing the good from our friendships requires intentionally carving out time to connect. As impersonal as it might sound to put friends on a schedule, if you land on specific times and rhythms to connect, it will help you avoid drifting apart.

Daily

Ironically, it's often the people who are in closest proximity to us that get the scraps for relational attention.

You know this. It's easy to reduce your connection with your spouse, kids, or extended family who live in the same house to logistical conversations about who needs to be where and at what time, who's going to make dinner on Thursday, or whose socks are on the floor instead of in the laundry.

It's critical to establish daily habits that make sure you connect with the people in your home, asking about the events of their day and how they were affected by them.

On my Refill Plan chart, I always put the words "Ask Nan" in my Relate/Daily box. Those words are literally there to remind me to ask Nan, my wife, how her day went and how it affected her. It probably doesn't earn me husband of the year honors that I have to put that on a chart, but it's helpful to have the constant reminder to connect with her daily about things more important than just logistics.

What kind of daily habits and routines could deepen your connection with those closest to you?

Weekly

Weekly rhythms of relational connection deepen your friendships with your inner circle. These are the people whom you could call if your car broke down or if you had a big personal win to celebrate.

Do you have friends like that?

Inviting some of our "functional" friends into regular times of connection can help superficial friendship turn into deeper, more meaningful friendship.

In Chapter Six, I told you about my group of friends who meet each week and are part of my "unpacking" strategy. While they are certainly helpful in talking about the heavy emotions that show up now and again, they're not just my emotional dumpster. They are my friends—guys I can count on, hang out with, laugh with, and trust deeply. Some I've known for more than twenty years. When one of my sons needs help and support, I'll often point them to one of these guys for perspective and wisdom. They are a treasure.

Those relationships deepened at weekly gatherings that included some food, drink, and funny, insightful, vulnerable, and at times sarcastic conversations. We're all better for the friendships we share.

What kind of weekly gathering could you invite some "functional" friends into that might turn into something more?

Monthly

Are there people you are close to but who don't live near you? You value their friendship and the connection you share, but they don't live near enough for you to get together regularly.

These are typically the people about whom we say, "We don't get together often enough." You don't because it's hard. They live in another town or way across town. The logistics of getting together in person can cause you to not get together at all if you're not careful.

I give friends who fit in this category a monthly phone call. I keep a list of these people to make sure I call them so we don't lose touch. I call them mostly when I'm driving. The fifteen or twenty minutes of a cross-town car trip provides a perfect amount of time to connect a bit each month and keep the relational drift from dragging us apart.

Who could you put on your monthly call list?

Periodically/Annually

You can use periodic or annual time frames to connect with family and friends who live farther away but are more important to you than just a phone call. You might target holidays and special occasions to stay connected and to possibly develop traditions that solidify those relationships.

My wife, Nan, has a group of girlfriends who met while living on the same wing of their college dorm. They set aside time each year to meet somewhere fun and pretty much talk the entire time. They'll do fun outings, but the bulk of time is spent in conversation about what's happening in each of the women's families. They prioritize staying connected in annual rhythms and have enjoyed the goodness of lifelong friendship.

Another way to use these longer time frames is to reconnect with old friends in other cities while you're traveling for work or on vacation. I have reconnected with a wide range of people—from my college roommate to friends I hadn't seen in over thirty years—simply by being proactive about looking them up and scheduling time to meet while I'm in their city. It's amazing how much life you can catch up on over an hour-and-a-half lunch.

There are people out there who have made your life richer and will make your life richer if you will slow down and prioritize time to connect.

Messy Goodness

Have you ever eaten a warm chocolate chip cookie?

You are missing out on the point of life if you haven't. There's nothing quite like the gooey richness of a thick, warm cookie that's got the right amount of crisp on the outside and soft, sugary, chocolatey goodness on the inside.

There's really only one problem (other than the potential sugar-induced health issues): you can't eat a cookie like that without making a mess. If you're eating them right, crumbs and chocolate get on everything. But if you're worried about the mess, you've probably missed the point. If you want the goodness of the cookie, you're going to have to get your hands dirty.

Aren't relationships like that? If you want the goodness, you're probably going to have to put up with a little mess here and there. But you are missing out on the point of life if you don't. We were created to live life in relationship with others.

Alone is always harder.

It might be more convenient and efficient to go it alone. You might even be able to move faster by yourself. But hear this clearly, from someone who prided himself in his solitude and independence (truthfully, hid himself in his solitude and independence): it is not better.

Sharing our experiences, accomplishments, sorrows, joys, challenges, laughter, pain, progress, and setbacks with dear, trusted friends makes life life.

Who do you need to invest in and enjoy more time with?

NOTES

[1] *Alone* (Leftfield Pictures, 2015–present).

[2] "New Surgeon General Advisory Raises Alarm about the Devastating Impact of the Epidemic of Loneliness and Isolation in the United States," US Department of Health and Human Services, May 3, 2023, https://www.hhs.gov/about/news/2023/05/03/new-surgeon-general-advisory-raises-alarm-about-devastating-impact-epidemic-loneliness-isolation-united-states.html.

[3] "New Surgeon General Advisory Raises Alarm."

[4] Dan Buettner, *The Blue Zones Secrets for Living Longer: Lessons from the Healthiest Places on Earth* (National Geographic, 2023), 210.

[5] National Academies of Sciences, Engineering, and Medicine, *Social Isolation and Loneliness in Older Adults: Opportunities for the Health Care System* (National Academies Press, 2020). https://doi.org/10.17226/25663.

[6] George Bagby, "Our Ruined Rivers," *Georgia Game and Fish*, November 1968.

10

Accidental Genius

I like working with good tools.

The best tools always help you do more than you could on your own. You're stronger with them than you are without them. They help you discover what's possible that wouldn't be without them. The best tools surprise you at how much help they offer if you'll just think about them a little more.

In 1948, a chemical compound was approved for use as a rodenticide, which is just a fancy way to say rat poison. It worked by causing massive internal bleeding in the unwanted rodents. The compound was first discovered in the 1920s as cattle and sheep that grazed on moldy sweet clover hay began to bleed to death after simple veterinary procedures. Seems the moldy hay contained an anticoagulant that was preventing blood of cattle and sheep from clotting. By 1940, scientists at the University of Wisconsin isolated the compound, patented it as a powerful anticoagulating drug, and named it after the Wisconsin Alumni Research Foundation, which funded its development. You might know this rodenticide today as the helpful, blood-thinning drug used to treat heart attacks, strokes, and blood clots: warfarin.

Cattle and sheep start dying, and it leads to saving human lives. I call that accidental genius.

Good tools become more helpful the more you know how to use them.

The Refill Plan will help you build an intentional strategy of rest, release, receiving, recreation, and relationships. It can be a powerful tool to help you move toward your true north and avoid early warning signs. You will get the replenishment you need to show up as your best self if you plot the five key habits in tandem with daily, weekly, monthly, periodic, and annual rhythms.

But as with any other tool, it will take time and practice to learn to use it well and get the most out of it. Not because the tool is complicated. It's not. It will take time and practice because you're complicated. Every one of us needs a plan as unique as we are.

To find the right mix and rhythms for your replenishment practices, you will need to reflect on what has been helpful to you in the past and what might be helpful now. As you figure that out, you'll be able to balance the stress and replenishment equation. It'll take some time to sort out. We'll discuss the role of self-awareness in our journey toward personal replenishment in the next chapter.

To make the most of the Refill Plan tool, here's what I suggest:

1. **Schedule a one-hour appointment with yourself to form a basic plan.** You'll need time to reflect on your current stresses and what kind of replenishing activities will restore what those stressors drain out. Don't rush through this. If an hour isn't enough, schedule more time. Starting well will help you benefit more quickly.

2. **Start small, and add as you go.** Begin with two or three practices you know have been helpful to you or that you are currently doing now. If you identify other activities as helpful and restorative, add those to your plan. As you try new habits and discover what works for you, add those along the way. But let me give you this warning: do not put anything on your plan that feels like drudgery! You may need to do those things, but this plan needs to be populated with habits that are life-giving, not soul-sucking.

3. **Put the plan on your calendar.** It's impossible to overstate the importance of this step. I've come to realize if something I want to do isn't on my calendar, it's imaginary. This plan must exist on your calendar, or it will probably never happen. I will say it this strongly: if you fail to put your Refill Plan activities on your calendar, you are no better off than someone who doesn't have a plan. You might actually be worse off because of the guilt you'll experience from creating a plan and not doing it. It may feel odd to put "Walk the dog" and "Reflect on what I'm carrying" on your calendar, but it will be more than worth the effort. Have I said it clearly enough? Put the plan on your calendar!

4. **Find your support.** Who could you recruit to be your ride-or-die when it comes to your replenishment plan? Others see us more clearly than we see ourselves. They will spot our early warning signs faster. They will notice how our depletion is affecting others around us before we will because they are the others who are around us. Your support people should be close enough to you to know your true north qualities and what they look like in practice. And they ought to be well acquainted with

your early warning signs and be both bold and gentle
enough to point them out in a way that helps and doesn't
harm you.

But Wait, There's More

As I began to use the plan to plot replenishing activities in the
right rhythms, I noticed some of my habits accomplished more
than one thing.

One of my great discoveries about what replenishes me is that
I need to change the scenery. Staycations do little for me, which
is interesting since I live in Las Vegas, where a lot of people go to
get away from work. I have friends who book a room at a local
resort and use their pool for a couple of days to relax. For whatever
reason, that doesn't work for me.

As I was building my plan for rest, I took the advice of my
counselor and invested in a couple of trips each year to Texas,
where my extended family lives. My uncle has a large ranch outside the small town where I was born, and he lets my brother and
me fish in his lakes. This seemed like a fantastic periodic rhythm
to help me shut off work and slow down. After a couple of trips, I
realized it did more for me than just provide downtime.

My brother and I bought a seriously janky plastic pontoon
boat that could easily be moved from one lake to another. We
would raid the local Walmart for fishing gear and boat accessories
before heading out to the lakes for a day on the water. Every time
we went out, it was an adventure. Some days we'd catch huge fish
that would have fed us and our families, and other days we'd just
feed the fish all our bait. Some days we'd be frustrated by the lack
of fish biting, and others we would talk so deeply about life that it
mattered little if we caught anything.

I discovered that my periodic rhythm of fishing was more than
just an escape from work. It was life-giving recreation and deeply

needed relational connection. It checked three boxes on my plan: rest, recreate, and relate.

A light came on.

Now that I knew what that periodic trip did for me, I could lean in to make sure I always received the full benefit of those three things. I soon noticed there were other practices that provided multiple benefits.

My day away from the office each month was certainly about rest, but I added the reflection and journaling exercise I described in Chapter Six and time fueling my purpose with podcasts and audio books.

The group of guys I'd get together with every month wasn't just about unpacking heavy emotions; it was also about enjoying the company of my friends.

Good tools become more helpful the more you know how to use them.

As I learned how to better use my Refill Plan tool, I started choosing different vacations. Previously, I planned what I thought was the standard, accepted form of vacation—go on a road trip, visit with family, go home. There's nothing wrong with visiting family on a vacation, and depending on the quality of your relationships with your family members, it can be very replenishing; it was for me. But it wasn't everything I needed from a vacation.

The Refill Plan helped me understand what made a great vacation for me. It wasn't only relational time with family and friends; I also needed downtime to rest, as well as have some time for fun and my version of adventure (seeing new things, enjoying new experiences, and visiting favorite places.) While that makes a great vacation for me, your ideal vacation may include inspirational activities that fuel your sense of purpose and calling—like going on a mission trip to a developing nation or visiting learning environments like museums or historical sites.

The five replenishing habits of rest, release, receive, recreate, and relate not only inform the kind of practices I need to balance stress and replenishment; they also act as a guide to define what I need from each of my replenishing practices.

Once you identify all that your replenishing practices can do for you, you can lean in to get the most out of what each activity offers.

This is part of the accidental genius of the Refill Plan.

Staying on Course

I discovered another accidental application of the Refill Plan the hard way—it helps you keep on track.

I didn't exactly ease into leading workshops on burnout and how to use this tool. I was still working my day job as the executive pastor of a large church while getting more and more calls to travel and speak all over the country. I quickly found myself on the road as a coach/consultant/speaker about half the time, learning to navigate the hazards of business travel while simultaneously trying to keep things at home and at my day job locked down.

I am not a multitasker. I'm more of a one-thing-at-a-time kind of guy. Doing two jobs was a lot for me, especially when the second job kept needing increasing amounts of time and attention.

I began to consider the irony of me burning out in the process of telling others how to not burn out. It was time to adjust my prescription and take a new dose of my own medicine. So I did what I encourage others to do. I used the Refill Plan.

I got my Refill Plan out and asked this insightful question: "What happened?" I know, it takes a genius to come up with something as brilliant as "What happened?" What I meant was: What had changed to cause me to feel so depleted? What caused my true north to fade and my early warning signs to flare? The plan that had been serving me well seemed to be failing me, so something must have shifted.

After studying the sheet for a while, it became clear. My day-away habit had gone missing for a couple of months because of all the travel. In the process of getting this new business running, I neglected a key piece of my plan. Truth is, I didn't know how key a role those days away played until I neglected them for a couple of months. When I did, the strain was obvious. The new level of activity added new stresses that needed the replenishment the day-away rhythms provided. Those days had become more essential because of the new weight I was carrying, and I had missed them completely. The plan showed me the error of my ways.

When I noticed the joy and peace of my true north slipping away, it provided me with a framework to assess why it was happening and what needed to change.

I once heard North Point Community Church pastor Andy Stanley say in a leadership talk, "You should always autopsy your success. If you don't know why you succeeded, you won't know how to fix it when it fails." I had experienced good days even when I was in the middle of burning out. There were even occasional days in that desperate time when I showed up with all the qualities of an eight. The problem was that I had no idea why. Because I didn't know why, I had nothing to guide me back onto the path when I was veering off course. I would think, "Maybe a week off will help?" But I had no real guidance.

When you put this plan in place, you'll discover it's not meant to be static. Life is dynamic, stressors change all the time, and your plan will have to adjust with it. The five R's and their accompanying rhythms become an assessment tool to help you adjust your plan to your changing circumstances.

Seasons Change

Not only will the demands and drains you're experiencing change, but different seasons of the year will require adjustments to your plan.

Have I mentioned that I love watching college football? When the fall season comes around, my recreational activity takes a turn in that direction. The only reason it's not on my plan all year is because I've been unable to convince the NCAA to play college football all year. (I'll let you know when they return my call.) Their current lack of cooperation with my replenishment needs means I have to adjust my plan during the spring and summer. Until I convince them otherwise, I'll be finding something else to do to fill that gap.

Also, I generally take two vacations per year—one in the summer, and another in the winter between Christmas and the New Year. The summer vacation is typically different than the one in winter. They require different amounts of time and planning. Because of these and other seasonal differences, my plan has to change throughout the year, and so will yours.

Taking the time to be proactive in making these kinds of adjustments is critical to staying on course. I find markers throughout the year that remind me it's time to refresh the plan and adjust it based on seasonal shifts or new needs that emerge. Currently, that means I'm adjusting my plan about three times each year. My markers are the start of the college football season (no, really), the start of the New Year (January 1), and the heat hitting Las Vegas (May). These are clear indicators to me that it's time for a change.

The replenishment plan doesn't serve you well if you let it grow stale. Keep it fresh, and it'll return the favor.

Genius Is in the Journey

The Refill Plan can do a lot for you, but it isn't magic.

Years ago, I gained quite a bit of weight. I had been busy raising kids and working at my job, and I had a lot of other excuses I could make up to explain why I had become so out of shape. My typical weight of 215 pounds had slowly crept up to nearly three hundred (I think—I wasn't exactly weighing myself every day), and I was starting to experience some health issues, like sleep apnea and back pain.

When I went to my doctor to get some help with the sleep problems, I thought he would prescribe sinus surgery to curb the apnea I was experiencing. My nose seemed pretty crooked—probably from playing high school and college football—and my self-diagnosis was that if he straightened it out, I'd be done with the snoring and apnea problems. It couldn't be that I was way overweight. The doctor, whom I knew from church, sent me to have a sleep study to see how bad the problem was.

It was worse than I thought.

At the follow-up appointment, my doctor friend told me I was waking up over fifty times an hour each night—which apparently isn't good for you. He went on to explain the kind of pressure that put on my heart and how the apnea was causing me to stop breathing for significant periods of time each night. Evidently, your brain and body don't work well without oxygen.

It was a little concerning. I proposed my "educated" solution to the doc of having sinus surgery to alleviate the issues I was having. What he told me was jarring to say the least.

"You don't have sinus problems. You're fat."

Um, excuse me?

"Lose forty or fifty pounds, and all of this goes away."

That day, a journey began that continues to this day.

Over the next eight months, I lost about seventy-five pounds (I think—I lost a few pounds before I was brave enough to get on the scale. When I finally did, it said 289.) I bottomed out back at my original weight of 215, and I've been working ever since to keep it under control. There are good days and bad, better seasons and worse. My weight goes up for a bit, and then I work at it to get it back down. I adjust my diet and my exercise to fit my life stage.

But I know that if I want to avoid the road I went down before, I can never stop checking the map and adjusting course.

There is no magic formula for being healthy.

The same goes for your replenishment.

Just like I've had to make some lifelong, course-altering choices about my physical health, I've also had to sign myself up for the long haul when it comes to my replenishment.

Let me share with you some inconvenient truths about the journey of keeping your tank full:

1. **You won't feel better right away.** If you commit to establishing and executing your Refill Plan, the results will not show up quickly. Just like with losing weight, you'll probably put in a fair amount of effort before the results you're hoping for will be easily noticeable. Remember, you can't force charge the batteries on your phone, and you can't force charge you. Work the plan. Give it time. Just because you don't feel better today doesn't mean it's not working. Besides, you need long-term life change, not quick-hit, temporary relief. This isn't about changing your destination; it's about going in a different direction, setting a new course for your life.

   My "goal" for my replenishment plan is: I want to be healthy (emotionally, physically, spiritually, etc.) for the rest of my life. Notice how that isn't a place I'll arrive? It's a journey I'm on.

   While you won't feel better immediately, you'll be growing healthier and stronger a little more every day.

The corollary to this is . . .

2. **You won't get stronger in a day.** Although you'll be growing stronger each day, lasting strength grows slowly over time. Some replenishing activities could help you change your mood a bit, but it may take some patience as you allow your resilience to increase.

    I've worked with people who started their plan, felt a little better, and went charging back into the same grind that depleted them in the first place. They discovered that full strength isn't recovered overnight.

    Just like with weight training, the longer you commit to your habits and rhythms, the more strength you'll gain.

    ► Your plan won't be perfect. Putting a good plan together will take some trial and error. You'll need to experiment with different reflection and unpacking strategies, times for rest, types of recreation, and how often you connect with the people in your life. You're also going to have to figure out the best length of time to try out each practice before you either adopt it long-term or ditch it for something better.

      The truth is, no plan is ever perfect. You will never stop needing to adjust the plan. You are changing. Your challenges are changing. The things that drain you and the things that restore you will change over time. Remember, you're trying to match your replenishment plan to the levels and types of stress you're experiencing. There's no such thing as the perfect plan.

    ► You'll be glad you did. Remember that thing we said about the best time to plant a tree? You can't go back thirty years (or thirty days for that matter) to start when you should have. But you can start today, and thirty years from now (or thirty days for that matter) you'll be glad you did. The only way you'll be glad later is by working the plan now.

Practical Genius

Working with any tool takes practice. But what's that thing they say about practice making . . . permanent? The more repetition and evaluated effort you bring to using any tool, the more effective you'll be and the more muscle memory you'll develop. You'll be able to do things with that tool someday that weren't possible before.

Even though the payoff won't be immediate, it will be significant. This is practical genius. And it's reserved for those who are willing to endure through the process of attempting, adjusting, adapting, and finally, advancing.

This is how discipline works. Discipline is all about enduring discomfort now so you can experience enjoyment later. You limit your freedom now so you can be truly free later. That's how almost every good thing arrives in your life. Good things come when you pay the price now so you can enjoy the benefits later. Bad things show up when you do the opposite—enjoy the benefits now and pay the price later. Debt works like that. Being overweight works like that. Burning out works like that.

I get it. Work can be fun. Accomplishments are exhilarating. Getting things done is satisfying. They can also wear you out.

Doing the work of using a new tool to build your plan might make you a little uncomfortable now, but when you see it starting to pay off, you'll be so glad you did.

11

Awareness Is Almost Everything

I never saw it coming.

We've all uttered those words at some point in our lives. It's the phrase we use when reality blindsides us, when our ability to predict the future fails spectacularly. The truth is, accurately foreseeing what's ahead is a challenge for all of us. You only have to watch the movie *Back to the Future* once to realize we have trouble seeing what's coming.

But it's not just the future that eludes us. Often, we struggle to grasp what's happening right now, especially when it comes to our own selves and what's happening around us. Self-awareness, it turns out, is tough.

Consider the proverbial frog in the kettle, oblivious to the gradually increasing water temperature, swimming around contentedly until it's too late. He never saw it coming.

A friend just shared with me about a time he was walking out of a hotel onto a city sidewalk while looking intently at his phone. He was trying to follow a map to his desired destination when, to his embarrassment and the amusement of everyone watching, he slammed into a parking meter, which knocked him to the ground and scattered everything he was carrying all over the sidewalk. He never saw it coming.

I gained eighty pounds and put my health in jeopardy. Didn't see it coming.

Burnout happens in much the same way. As I mentioned in earlier chapters, I considered myself the least likely candidate for burnout. I didn't see it coming because I was looking in the other direction. I was keeping my eye on an organization, family, finances, responsibilities. I was watching problems, people, and plans in every direction. But I wasn't watching me.

More accurately, I had a blind spot when it came to assessing my own well-being. I was barely aware of my feelings, let alone how I was doing. I didn't have a gauge that told me how close I was to running out of fuel. It's like I was driving along with a broken gas gauge thinking, *There must be fuel in the tank because I'm still moving.* Little did I know I was only moving because I was headed downhill.

From the frog in the kettle to my friend hitting the parking meter, from my weight getting out of control to my burnout—all could have been avoided by doing one simple thing.

Paying attention.

This is why this may be the most important chapter in the whole book. When it comes to beating burnout and showing up as the best version of you, self-awareness is almost everything.

I say "almost" because you still need the tools we've discussed, and you'll still need to intentionally build a plan of helpful habits and rhythms. But when it comes to personal replenishment, there might not be a more important competency to develop than a keen awareness of what is going on inside of you. There also may not be a harder quality to develop.

Eyes on the Target

There are, throughout the Refill Plan, important markers to keep an eye on. I've pointed them out along the way, but I want to collect them all here.

The most critical indicator to familiarize yourself with is your true north, which is made up of the two or three qualities that describe you at your very best. Your true north is the guidepost against which you measure how full your tank truly is. You should not only know what these qualities are; you should be well acquainted with how they feel.

Take a moment to visualize the last time you felt truly great:

- ▶ Your tank was full.
- ▶ Your eyes were bright.
- ▶ You felt rested and ready to go.

Let that feeling sink in. You want that experiential memory to not only be a goal but to become your guide. The more aware you are of what your true north feels like, the more you'll recognize the next time the needle starts slipping toward depletion.

Do you remember what rested and replenished feels like to you? Go back: you may need to go way back and sit with those feelings for a minute. Close your eyes, and remember that vacation at the beach where you felt completely relaxed or that week at work when you were hitting on all cylinders. That is you at your best. Your awareness of how that feels will be to you what magnetic north is to a compass.

Running a close second to knowing your true north is being acutely aware of your early warning signs. These blinking red lights on your personal dashboard are often the first indicators that you are drifting from your true north.

During the early days of my recovery from burnout, I watched these signs like a hawk. I didn't want to slip back into the patterns that caused my crash. The minute I noticed irritation or anxiety starting to peep out from behind the bushes, I would address it immediately by asking, "What is happening to cause this?" and "What can I do to address it?" If I caught myself engaging in negative self-talk ("You're an idiot. C'mon Mitch! What's wrong with you?"), I'd stop whatever I was doing and address it immediately.

Throughout this process, I learned a crucial lesson: the more aware I became of my true north and early warning signs, the quicker I could address depletion and find recovery.

What Helps

While your true north and early warning signs help you focus on your ultimate goal, your stress/replenishment scale keeps you balanced as you pursue the goal of being at an eight 80 percent of the time.

Stress/replenishment awarenesses work together. The more you understand what is causing your stress, the clearer you'll be about how to diffuse it. This synergy is crucial for maintaining balance and avoiding burnout.

Before I played football at the four-year college level, I played for a junior college team that was blessed with an amazingly talented and caring athletic trainer. Fred's job was to tape and rehab our strained and injured team back to health so we'd be ready for the game next weekend. Anytime a player would go to Fred with an injury, the first thing he would do is fold his arms and ask questions. A lot of questions. But after the questions came the part that made him a good trainer. It was the "Does this hurt?"

test. Fred would start poking and twisting the injured appendage, and with each move he would ask, "Does this hurt?" Most of the time, he barely got the question out before a yelp of pain told him all he needed to know. Fred's genius lay in his ability to accurately diagnose the source of pain, allowing him to apply the most effective treatment.

Before you can know what replenishing habits need to be a part of your plan, you need to sharpen your understanding of the types of stress you're experiencing. Start by asking yourself probing questions like:

- ▶ What am I afraid of?"
- ▶ "What am I carrying?"
- ▶ "What wears me out?"

These questions will help you unpack what's happening in the moment that stresses you out and will also give you clues to the types of recovery activities you'll need.

If, for example, your stress comes from constantly living under the ticking clock of deadlines, your replenishment may need to be marked by minimal scheduled activities and few demands on your time. On the other hand, if your stress comes from constant decision-making, particularly the kind that impacts a lot of people, you may need the kind of time off that requires few decisions. You might want to vacation in familiar spots where you've established well-worn paths, or you may want someone else to plan the trip for you and invite you along for the ride.

Gaining awareness of the types of replenishment needed to match the kind of stress you experience will take some reflection and experimentation. But the more aware you become, the more skilled you'll be in maintaining this all-important balance.

Plans Change

You will also need to stay aware of when your Refill Plan (including the five R's: rest, release, receive, recreate, and relate) will need a refresh. And yes, your plan will need a refresh. Life is dynamic, and what works today may not be as effective tomorrow. Recognizing the need for periodic updates is key to maintaining a robust and relevant Refill Plan.

One of the questions I get asked the most in my workshops is, "How often will I need to redo my plan?" My best answer is, "When your current plan isn't as helpful as it was." That answer may seem frustratingly nonspecific, but it highlights a critical skill: the ability to recognize when your strategies are losing their effectiveness. This awareness is a cornerstone of maintaining a vibrant Refill Plan.

I typically refresh my plan about three times a year. I set aside specific time to reflect on where I've been and to build a new plan. I'll sometimes use a simple template:

- ► Look back
- ► Look around
- ► Look ahead

I look back at where I've been to assess what's been particularly helpful or unhelpful in getting me to my true north. I identify patterns in my stress that have triggered my early warning signs.

Then I'll look at my current situation to evaluate where I am on the scale and to see if there are any new realities I might need to account for in my updated plan.

Finally, I'll look ahead for issues, obstacles, or challenges that might require an adjustment, or if there are opportunities for replenishment that weren't available in the previous season (like college football games or holiday breaks.)

While the mechanics of refreshing your plan are important, the real secret lies in your awareness. It's about developing the insight to recognize when your plan needs a reboot. This awareness ensures your plan remains fresh and continues to serve you well.

Heads-Up Display

I was driving a rental car to a speaking engagement and noticed it had a feature I'd heard of but never seen before: a heads-up display.

Right there projected on the lower part of the windshield was the speed of the vehicle and a couple of other helpful indicators that would normally have only shown up on the "old-fashioned" dashboard below.

I loved it. It felt like I was flying a spaceship. (Can you tell I'm easily impressed?)

I'm well aware that the point of the heads-up display is to keep drivers' eyes on the road while providing access to essential driving data. It's a brilliant solution to a common problem: how to stay informed without getting distracted. But I must confess I was so captivated by the little numbers on the windshield and how it worked that I almost crashed the car. (I know there might be something wrong with me.)

Even though I may have missed the point of the cool instruments in the rental car, the purpose of them was not lost on me. It's a good idea to watch your gauges as you navigate the twists and turns coming at you. Things change quickly, and you need to know how to adjust with them. Gauges build awareness.

The Dashboard

As I reflected on the path that led to my burnout, a pattern emerged. I would go out the door in the morning, brimming with energy and all the best intentions, only to return home with the worst attitude and depleted of energy because of the challenges I faced that day.

The problem? I lacked a way to monitor how I was responding to the events of the day. Without that awareness, those events would often get the best of me, leaving others to get the worst of me. As I learned more about how personal replenishment works, I realized the need for a way to monitor and adjust how I was doing in the middle of the hustle that day.

That realization led to the creation of the personal dashboard—a heads-up display designed to keep us from veering off into the ditches of burnout.

Just as every car with an internal combustion engine has four essential gauges on its dashboard, I identified four critical indicators to help monitor the vital functions that keep us running toward our true north all day.

The Speedometer: Your External Pace

In the same way the speedometer on your car tells you about the external speed of your vehicle, you should monitor your personal speedometer to create awareness of your external pace. In other words, you should ask yourself how fast you're going in the process of getting it all done. You've had those days when you explain your

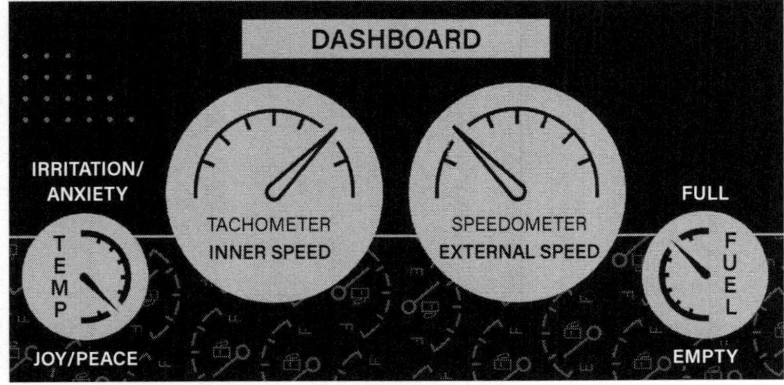

pace by saying, "Man, I've been running all day!" Yeah, me too. You find yourself six or seven back-to-back appointments deep and know you've just joined the office running club. Parents who double as the household taxi service for kids who need to be at school, then soccer, then piano lessons, and then the dentist know what daily speed is all about.

There's nothing necessarily wrong with occasionally running fast. But beware "speed wobble"—when your pace becomes unsustainable. Ever watch a little kid run down a hill and lose their balance? Their body starts moving faster than their legs can keep up, and a face-plant becomes inevitable. Paying attention to how fast you're running can help you keep your emotional and mental feet under you as you navigate your day.

The Tachometer: Your Internal RPMs

The tachometer in your car measures its engine speed, and this gauge measures your internal RPMs: your mental and emotional state.

You know what I'm talking about. We've all experienced our internal engine getting wound up as the pressures of the day mounted or the pace of the day picked up. I can get internally spun up even when I don't have a lot going on. All I have to do is feel like there's a lot or something big going on, and my mind races, taking my pulse with it. This is what hypertension—or high blood pressure—is all about: pressure on the outside causing pressure on the inside.

Here's the cool thing: your car can separate its external speed from its engine speed. That's why your car can go eighty-five mph (but please drive the posted speed limit) down the freeway with your RPMs relatively low. How? Your car finds another gear. So can you. When I notice myself heading into a day where I need to move fast or a day that has pressure points in it, I'll tell myself,

"Walk slowly through this fast day." I'll take a couple of deep breaths to help me turn my internal engine speed down and then monitor my inner tachometer throughout the day.

Again, it's all about awareness.

The Temperature Gauge: Your Emotional State

If you don't know much about engines, the temperature gauge might seem superfluous. I mean, what do I care what temperature my engine is running at? But heat build-up can be the worst enemy of an engine that derives its power from controlled explosions. Overheating can do irreparable damage to an engine, rendering a vehicle useless to do what it was intended to do.

In the same way, heat build-up can cause irreparable damage both inside you and to relationships with those around you. It can be your worst enemy if you plan to stay away from burnout.

On my personal temperature gauge:

▶ "Running hot" equates to my early warning signs: irritation and anxiety.

▶ "Running cool" represents my true north qualities: joyfulness and peace.

Before I used these gauges to build my awareness, I paid little attention to what my internal temperature was doing during the course of a day. I'm sure others noticed.

Some days, my temperature would get out of control because I was running fast and I had allowed my internal RPMs to get spun up. From there, it would take very little in the way of work-related speed bumps or figurative (and sometimes literal) "slow drivers" in my lane to get me overheated. Other days, it happened the other way around. I'd get irritated by something at the start of the day—the kids, the car, the dog, the deadline, whatever—and in the wake of my rising temperature, my engine speed would soon be revving out of control, and my external speed would soon follow. I'd be moving fast and feeling amped, all because of an irritation that set me off.

Ever been there?

Regular temperature checks can help you make necessary adjustments before you overheat.

The Fuel Gauge: Your Energy Level

The final gauge represents your energy level, which is impacted by all the other factors—external speed, internal RPMs, and core temperature. A person running "fast and hot" burns through their fuel much quicker than one operating under control.

It's dangerously easy to start your day with a full tank, only to burn through it all before you leave the office or finish your tasks for the day. The result? You have nothing left for the people and activities that matter most in your life.

Using these gauges to build awareness allows you to make real-time adjustments, keeping your tank full for the things that truly matter.

The Dashboard—Adjustment

We've established that awareness is almost everything when it comes to preventing burnout. Why almost? Because of the crucial step that follows awareness: your response.

Noticing what's happening is the first step. The key to lasting change is in how we adjust based on that awareness. It's one thing to realize you're overheating; it's another to cool down.

Here's a critical distinction: your personal gauges are like thermometers, not thermostats.

- ► Thermometers measure the current temperature. They provide information but don't control the environment.

> ▶ Thermostats not only measure but also regulate temperature, automatically making adjustments to maintain a set point.

Your personal gauges—speedometer (pace), tachometer (internal RPMs), temperature gauge (emotional state), and fuel gauge (energy level)—all serve the same function as a thermometer. They tell you what's happening, but they don't control it.

These gauges are invaluable tools for information; taking the initiative to change what's happening is the next step.

How do you do it?

Adjusting your Speed

If you want to adjust your external speed, adjust your calendar. Take some time to reflect on how many appointments you can do in a day and not develop speed wobble. Come up with a number—is it six, seven, four?—and then subtract one. You need to leave some margin for the unexpected and unplanned speed bumps and traffic jams you'll encounter in your day.

If you work in an office setting, make every meeting you schedule fifty minutes or less instead of the standard one-hour timeframe. You can't always control the length of meetings others set, but you can control yours. Be disciplined about wrapping up with at least ten minutes left in the hour, and then use that time to recalibrate your speed in preparation for the next meeting. Go ahead and use that extra ten minutes (or more) to adjust all your gauges. Couldn't hurt, right?

Don't miss this: you have more control over your calendar than you think you do.

Read that again.

Our calendars are a record of decisions we have made about how we use our time. I know it's easy to think that other people have set the agenda for us, but we let them. We decided to work at that job. We decided to sign the kids up for all those sports teams and activities. And there's nothing wrong with that. But knowing that allows us to recommit to the decisions we have already made—"Those meetings are a chance to express my purpose through my work. Let's go!"—rather than feel like we're a victim. The energy shift is amazing when we reframe our calendar as commitments rather than inconveniences.

Beyond work, we also have control over how we use our non-working hours. I've talked to many who try to balance fast-paced work weeks with fast-paced "recreation" activities on the weekend, only to end up more tired.

Speed requires energy. So use your calendar to carve out slower times of recharging so you can go fast when it's required, and avoid the speed wobble that can cause a crash.

Adjusting your Inner RPMs

Your inner engine speed is driven by a single, powerful force: intensity. The more tense or intense you become, the higher your inner RPMs will climb.

Don't get me wrong: there are times when a heightened state of intensity is a good thing.

Recently, in my wife's work as an American Sign Language interpreter, she was called on to provide interpretation services for a group of deaf and hard-of-hearing people on a visit to a local tourist spot. Suddenly, a person from another group nearby was overcome by the heat of the day and passed out, hitting their head hard enough to cause everyone around to gasp. While some from their group rushed to the aid of this person, a worker at the attraction looked over, saw what was happening, and in a way that sounded like Eeyore responding to a bother, said, "I'll go find some help" and slowly walked away.

A little more intensity would have been helpful.

However, more often than not, our struggle with intensity stems from bringing an excess of it into situations that don't warrant it. There's actually a technical term for that. It's called "parents at a Little League Baseball game." Have you ever seen those parents? Have you ever been those parents? Something happens when ten-year-olds play baseball that makes it hard for some adults to stay calm.

Intensity is not necessarily anger. Let's call it "over-amped energy." It's often aggressive even when it's not angry. You may have witnessed the excited intensity of a herd of people waiting to get into a concert that almost tramples people near to death in their exuberance-turned-impatience to get to their seat. Their intensity isn't based in anger, but it's only a short trip from ecstatic to enraged. Intensity is easily combustible.

If you want to manage your inner RPMs effectively, you must learn to adjust your intensity. This takes an enormous amount of self-awareness. To make corrections, you need to not only to see how intense you are in the moment, but you also need to recognize why. When you see your intensity gauge creeping up toward the red line, ask yourself, "What pressure am I feeling right now?" Intensity increases in response to perceived pressure. Recognizing what's pushing you, demanding of you, or challenging you can go a long way toward reigning in your inner acceleration.

Lowering your Temperature

Of all the gauges we've discussed, the temperature gauge—our emotional state—might be the most challenging to adjust. Once our temperature gauge starts moving north, it's hard to walk it back.

But it is possible.

One day not long ago, I was heading to the Las Vegas airport to catch a plane to Atlanta for a speaking engagement. My car was in the shop, so I was in an Uber, cruising south on Interstate 15 through the middle of the city. It was a typical busy mid-morning, but traffic was moving smoothly.

Suddenly, several Highway Patrol vehicles showed up out of nowhere, lights flashing, and began weaving back and forth to slow traffic. Within minutes, all six lanes of traffic ground to a dead stop. Of course, I was wondering what was going on. Sometimes when the president would come to town, roads would get blocked off to safeguard the motorcade, but I hadn't heard anything about a presidential visit. We were just sitting there.

Five minutes passed.

Then ten.

I kept glancing at my watch, calculating the time I would have to navigate security so I could make my flight.

Twelve minutes.

Fifteen minutes.

What do you suppose was happening to my internal temperature gauge? If you guessed I was running cool and keeping the needle pegged on my joyful, peaceful true north, you'd be very wrong. I was not cool.

Finally, out of the corner of my eye, I spotted a long procession of emergency vehicles passing on the right side of the road. Rescue vehicles, ambulances, motor cops, even Department of Forestry trucks—pretty much every official vehicle in the county with a light on top was in this mile-long convoy. And then I remembered.

A month earlier, two young highway patrol officers had pulled over in the middle of the night to help a stranded motorist right near where we were on Interstate 15. A drunk driver ran over and killed both officers, robbing two families of husbands and fathers. It was all over the news. Our whole city mourned.

The long line of emergency vehicles passing on the highway was the funeral procession for one those officers whose memorial service was scheduled for that day. We weren't just stuck in traffic; we were sitting there to honor his life and show respect to his family.

What do you think happened to my temperature gauge when I realized that?

Right.

I told my Uber driver, "I'll miss my plane for this."

If you want to adjust your temperature gauge, here's the secret: add some perspective.

That day, I got a full dose of perspective. Now, whenever I feel my irritation or anxiety levels rising, I remind myself that whatever is bothering me might not be as significant as it seems in the moment.

It's all about how you perceive the situation.

Remember the last time you were running hot? Did anything good come from that? Were you proud of the way you showed up? Did others have a good experience interacting with you? Were you happy about the outcomes?

I know I'm leaning hard on this one, but anger is so dangerous. I've said it before in early chapters; anger is like a fire—potentially useful if contained, but it rarely stays controlled. And once it's out of control, it burns things to the ground. More damage has been done to relationships because of anger than perhaps any other single factor.

In the New Testament, James, the half brother of Jesus, offers this sobering warning: "Human anger does not produce the righteousness God desires" (James 1:20 NLT). You may not be a religious person or care much about what God desires. I'm not here to convince you to think otherwise. But we can all learn something from this straightforward caution: good doesn't come from anger. Truth is, anger won't produce the kind of life you desire either.

Perhaps the reason James felt compelled to write this was because, deep down, many of us believe the opposite. I had to eventually admit that I thought my anger would correct my kids' disobedience, let others know their behavior was unacceptable, and motivate people to be more productive.

I was wrong.

If you're committed to adjusting your temperature to avoid boiling over and damaging your inner well-being and relationships:

- Pause: when you feel your temperature rising, take a moment before reacting.
- Breathe: take some deep, slow breaths to help calm your physiological response.
- Pray: invite a new perspective that will help you stay cool when the heat is on.

Empty or Full?

When you effectively use the gauges on your personal dashboard—adjusting your speed, inner RPMs, and temperature—you'll notice a direct impact on your fuel gauge.

Your fuel gauge isn't just another indicator—it's the culmination of all your efforts in self-management. It reflects your current capacity to handle the challenges and opportunities that lie ahead. Here's why it's so critical:

- Daily fluctuations, long-term impact: While your fuel levels can change from day to day, the cumulative effect of these daily variations determines your long-term resilience or susceptibility to burnout.

- ► Gradual nature of burnout: Burnout doesn't typically occur overnight. It's the result of consistent depletion over time without adequate replenishment.
- ► Incremental improvements matter: Each day, you're either burning down a little more or filling up, depending on the adjustments you've made. These small daily changes can lead to significant long-term outcomes.

Add the awarenesses this dashboard offers to your understanding of your true north, early warning signs, and sense of when your plan needs a refresh, and you'll give yourself the best chance to make the adjustments needed to keep your tank full.

Your level of self-awareness is the competency that makes a full tank possible.

Mirror Holders

There's a caveat to everything I just wrote about developing self-awareness: no matter how self-aware you are, you're not as good at seeing yourself as others are.

Sorry to be the one to tell you.

Yes, you should work on it. Yes, you should use these tools. Yes, you can improve—give your wholehearted effort to trying to get better at it. But you're never going to be as good at seeing yourself as you think you are.

I once took an emotional intelligence test, and my highest score by far was my self-awareness. When I saw that, I laughed out loud. Why? Because my life had been marked by a continual string of conversations that all led to me apologizing: "Man, I'm really sorry. I didn't think I was coming across that way."

I don't see myself very clearly.

Neither do you.

This isn't a personal failing on our part; it's rooted in our biology and psychology. We suffer from:

- ▶ Proximity bias: we're too close to ourselves to maintain objectivity. Just as you can't focus on something held directly in front of your eyes, it's challenging to see yourself clearly.
- ▶ Cognitive biases: our brains are wired with numerous biases that distort our self-perception, such as the self-serving bias and confirmation bias.
- ▶ Emotional involvement: our emotions can cloud our judgment, especially when it comes to self-evaluation.
- ▶ Lack of context: we're present for all our thoughts and actions, but we lack the external context of how these appear to others.

As we're told in Scripture, "The heart is deceitful above all things and beyond cure. Who can understand it" (Jer. 17:9)? Do you know what this means? There is something inside of you that is not just blind to the truth, but it's intentionally trying to deceive you. You don't even have to believe the Bible to know it's true.

We need help. We need mirror holders. These are the brave souls willing to hold up a mirror so we can take an unvarnished look at ourselves. They help us to see how we're really doing. They can see our early warning signs long before we do. You might walk into a room thinking, *I'm not really myself today. I'm a little less present, positive, and patient than I'd like to be.* They see you walk in and think, *Wow. You're kind of distracted, irritated, and impatient today.* Make no mistake: they are right, and you are not.

It's not because you're dull or intentionally obtuse. It's because no one sees things well when they're too close to them, and there is no one closer to you than you. Mirror holders love you and are just far enough away to see you as you really are. Sure, they can be mistaken, but they are rarely wrong about how you're coming across to others, because they are one of the others. Because they care, they're willing to provide this crucial feedback to your face. I heard someone say, "A real friend is someone who will stab you in the front." Painful as it might be, you need a few, trusted friends like that.

If you're serious about enhancing your self-awareness and preventing burnout, here's how to leverage the power of mirror holders:

- ► Identify your mirror holders: choose a few people who know you well, care about you deeply, and have the courage to be honest.
- ► Share your dashboard: explain your personal dashboard, including your early warning signs and the gauges you're trying to monitor.
- ► Grant permission: give them explicit permission to provide feedback when they notice changes in your behavior or demeanor.
- ► Commit to non-defensiveness: promise you won't argue or disagree with their observations.
- ► Express gratitude: always thank them for their feedback, even (especially) when it's hard to hear.
- ► Reflect and act: use their observations as a starting point for deeper self-reflection and making positive changes.

Let's be honest: their observations will be mildly annoying at first. Okay, they'll never stop being mildly annoying. But that discomfort is a small price to pay for the insights you'll gain.

Each time you receive feedback and pause to reassess and adjust, you are taking another crucial step toward burnout-proofing your life.

12

Good Living, Great Life

Look at your life. Look at your choices.

Words to live by. One afternoon, they became the center of a memory we still talk about in our family.

We were having one of those dinners you don't get to have very often. Special place. Unique time. Our kids at just the right age to appreciate the rarity of the occasion.

I had surprised the kids with an unexpected stop at Disneyland during a family vacation. They had no idea we were going until we were almost there. Our family loves Disneyland (I can understand if yours doesn't), so it's always a big deal when we can make it happen.

This time, I decided to splurge on some things we didn't normally get to do, including dinner reservations at the Blue Bayou. If you're not familiar, the Blue Bayou is the restaurant you pass in your boat as you enter the Pirates of the Caribbean attraction. Set in the New Orleans Square section of Disneyland, it's an immersive experience with a swampy, dimly lit environment, Creole- and

Cajun-inspired décor, and food that takes you straight to the heart of the South.

Our waiter, Josh, was fantastic even by the high standards of Disneyland. His friendliness and dry sense of humor quickly endeared him to our crew.

Adding to the ambiance in the restaurant was a small glass lantern on our table, its candle providing a warm glow. Our youngest son, Jacob, was fascinated by it. That's a polite way of saying: he kept goofing around with it as we waited for Josh to return with our beverages. We told him to quit messing with it—even Josh the waiter had playfully admonished him—but his curious nature wouldn't let him leave it alone.

As the rest of us chatted and admired the scenery, we were suddenly plunged into darkness, as if someone had turned off a light. Yes, you know why. Jacob had "accidentally" blown out the candle. The absence of that tiny flame was surprisingly noticeable in the already dim room.

Just as we turned to scold Jacob, Josh reappeared with our drinks, a perfectly timed faked scowl, and some words of wisdom for our son: "Look at your life. Look at your choices."

We all had a good laugh, and it created an unforgettable family moment. As Josh relit the candle, he couldn't have known how appropriate those words were for the one son whose all-out, go-fast, gregarious nature often led him at times to act first and think about outcomes later—always with a smile on his face.

From that day forward, whenever Jacob would come home with skinned knees, a bump on his head, and a story to tell, we'd repeat Josh the waiter's sage counsel: "Look at your life. Look at your choices."

It's not bad advice for all of us.

Look at Your Life

These days, I spend a lot of my time speaking and leading workshops for people who are working hard to make a good living. Some are even making what could be described as a great living. I deeply appreciate those who work hard to make a living and run businesses that create job opportunities for others.

I was raised with a strong work ethic by parents who stayed in their respective careers for thirty-five years—my mom as an elementary school teacher, and my dad as the senior executive of a government agency. They taught my brother and me by example that hard work and perseverance are key to earning a good living. You might share these values.

I'd bet the reason you've read this book is because you have the value of hard work embedded deep within you. You're pursuing a great living through meaningful work, whether it's in the home, the marketplace, or a church or nonprofit. You worked hard and have experienced some of the rewards generated by that effort.

Here's what concerns me most, and it's why I do the work I do: it's very possible that after working hard to make a good living, you end up with a miserable life to show for it.

That would be such a shame.

The best sermon I ever heard on personal replenishment was from Lance Witt, who used to be the executive pastor at Saddleback Church, working with Rick Warren for years. Lance is a great speaker, leader, and author, and he literally wrote *the* book on personal replenishment: *Replenish*—you should get a copy and read it sometime.

Lance said maybe we unintentionally end up with a miserable life after working so hard because we've bought the lie that says, *The price you have to pay for the good life is the bad life.*

You might want to read that one more time.

You know what he means, right? Somewhere along the way, you might have started believing the best things in life are only available if you work yourself to death to get them. Go hard at it sixty hours a week at work, never turn off your laptop, run yourself ragged as you make sure the kids do every activity under the Sun while maintaining the highest GPA in their class, go to the gym, serve on the school board, volunteer at church, make sure your house is spotless and looks like an HGTV renovation just happened, optimize your investments, walk your dog, take care of your yard, turn in that proposal, and whatever you do, never, under any circumstances, shut off your phone, because you might miss something important.

Then you'll have the good life.

Do you see the problem with that?

Maybe it's time we redefine what we mean by "the good life."

Back to True North

I had you begin your journey by identifying your true north, because when you described yourself on your best day, you described the good life.

You described a life that is:

- Peaceful
- Patient
- Positive
- Present
- Productive
- Purposeful

(I'm not sure why all these start with the letter "P." Draw your own conclusions.)

Other true north words most likely fit into one of those six "P" categories:

- ► Focused
- ► Optimistic
- ► Energized
- ► Clear
- ► Engaged
- ► Helpful
- ► Unhurried
- ► Just plain happy

All of these are subsets of those "P" words.

What you said, in essence, is that the good life is not about what you get. It's about who you are.

It's not about having the good life.

It's about living a good life.

As a follower of Jesus, I can't help but point out that Jesus's stated purpose for his life was, at least in part, to offer a different quality of living to anyone who chose to follow him. Jesus came as both an example and an invitation to experience the life God had originally intended for his creation. This profound offer was beautifully expressed by Jesus: "The thief's purpose is to steal and kill and destroy. My purpose is to give them a rich and satisfying life" (John 10:10 NLT).

Jesus acknowledges the existence of forces that can rob you of the fullness your life was meant to include. Then he points to a different version of "the good life"—a rich and satisfying life that he not only lived but shared with others. Accessing this life of abundance requires a shift in perspective and priorities. It requires you to leave behind the mad pursuit of the kind of gain that will ultimately diminish you, and it calls for you to aim your life in the direction of another.

Jesus understood that you can spend your life trying to make a great living, lose sight of the goodness of life, and chase material success at the expense of spiritual wealth. He cautioned, "And what do you benefit if you gain the whole world but lose your own soul? Is anything worth more than your soul" (Matt. 16:26 NLT)?

The answer to that question, by the way, is no.

Nothing is worth more than your soul.

Just ask anyone who's lost it for a while.

Jesus is trying to wave us all off the path that would promise us great gain but eventually deliver nothing.

This is why it's essential to know your true north and the path to get there.

The activities on your Refill Plan are not just a means to an end. They are opportunities to engage the journey and enjoy friends, God, family, meaningful work, and, ultimately, your life along the way. It isn't a checklist or another to-do list; it's a vehicle to help you recapture the life that stress, pressure, and unrealistic goals and demands want to steal away.

The Refill Plan is meant to create eddies in the current of your daily, weekly, monthly, periodic, and annual rhythms that allow you to slow down and find fulfillment rather than letting the rush of life's rapids whisk you downriver so quickly that you miss the best parts of the journey.

It's meant to help you slow down and soak in the good life.

Look at Your Choices

The biggest objection I get to the Refill Plan comes in many forms, but they're all really just different ways of saying the same thing. I've heard it from business leaders, stay-at-home parents, church leaders, blue collar workers, and retirees alike. At some point, we've all probably told ourselves some version of this story: "I'm too busy to rest."

My answer is always the same: "You're probably right."

The trap nearly everyone falls into is thinking their circumstances dictate that response. They don't. Your circumstances might demand a response, but they don't get to say what it will be.

Only you get to do that.

You get to choose.

I know there are bills to be paid, but you still get to decide the level at which you'll live and what you'll do to generate the income to live that way. Yes, there are kids to raise. But you still get to choose how many activities they'll participate in at any one time. Yes, life throws us curveballs, like breast cancer, layoffs, recessions, and inflation, but you still get to choose your perspective.

You get to choose:

- ► How you'll show up.
- ► How much you need to have.
- ► Where you'll work (or won't work.)
- ► How much attention you'll give to your replenishment.

You get to choose whether you'll set your personal compass toward your true north or not.

Maybe Josh was right: Look at your life. Look at your choices.

Here's a hard truth we all get to live with: replenishment is 100 percent your responsibility.

When I burned out, I was embarrassed and wanted to blame others. In reality, it was my adaptive challenges and poor choices that created the downward spiral. Sure, there were pressures and tough circumstances, but ultimately, the real problem was me.

While this plan isn't a cure-all for everything draining you, it can be a guide to help you write your own prescription for personal health. It'll support you as you make a good living, but more importantly, it will help you have more life.

Burnout is a self-inflicted wound.

You can make a different choice.

You can decide who you want to be.

This Is Your Life

In 2003, alternative rock band Switchfoot produced a soul-stirring album, *The Beautiful Letdown*, that included the song "This Is Your Life." The penetrating chorus challenges us with these words:

> This is your life,
> are you who you want to be?
> This is your life,
> is it everything you dreamed that it would be
> When the world was younger,
> and you had everything to lose?[1]

Great questions:

- Are you who you want to be?
- Is your life what you dreamed?
- How does your current reality compare to what you imagined your life would be some day?

Those questions are meant as an invitation, not an indictment. They're meant to stir reflection and rethinking, not regret.

Remember, you still get to choose. It's never too late to set a course toward true north.

My hope is that you'll choose a life in which joy and peace fill your tank to overflowing.

NOTE

[1]Switchfoot, "This Is Your Life," track 2 on *The Beautiful Letdown*, Columbia/Sony BMG, 2003.